D1636569

Santería:

AFRICAN MAGIC IN LATIN AMERICA

MIGENE GONZÁLEZ-WIPPLER

Original Publications
New York

Santeria: African Magic in Latin America was originally published in hardcover edition by The Julian Press, Inc. (Crown Publishers) in 1973. First paperback edition published in 1974 by Doubleday. Subsequent editions published by Original Publications.

First edition published 1981
Second printing 1984
Third printing 1987
Fourth printing 1988
Fifth printing 1989
Sixth printing 1990

Second revised edition 1992

ISBN 0-942272-04-08

ORIGINAL PUBLICATIONS
22 East Mall
Plainview, New York 11803
(516) 454-6809

WWW.ORIGINALPUBLICATIONS.COM

Contents

Preface

The first edition of *Santería: African Magic in Latin America* was first written in 1972 and published in 1973. The first publisher I submitted the manuscript to was Doubleday, who promptly turned it down on the grounds that the subject matter was "too specialized" for their list. Many other publishers rejected the manuscript also, approximately twenty in total. I could have literally papered my wall with the rejection slips. Then, a sensitive publisher with a vision by the name of Arthur Ceppos, read the book, loved it and decided to publish it. The name of his publishing company was Julian Press, which was later to become part of the Crown Publishing Group.

Julian Press was a very small company, publishing only three to four books a year. But each of those books was a small jewel. Among the famous authors who were first published by Julian Press were John Lilly and Ron L. Hubbard, whose now classic *Dianetics* was a Julian Press original hardcover. And much of the fame now enjoyed by these and other authors was due to the tenacity and the development power of Arthur Ceppos. Arthur — was and is — a unique individual, someone relentlessly driven by a thousand demons, each of them obsessed by a thirst for perfection. This constant drive reflected itself in Arthur's relationships with his authors, each of whom he prodded mercilessly, searching for hidden wisdoms, for additional mind matter to add to an already meticulously edited and revised manuscript. Arthur was not only publisher, he was editor, agent, friend and Spanish inquisitor all rolled into one. Everything I have ever written and everything I may still write has been and will be deeply influenced by that sartorial mind of impeccable and implacable judgment.

Santería: African Magic in Latin America was Arthur Ceppos' accomplishment. I only wrote the book, he created it. And the mark of his brilliance is so firmly stamped on the book, that even though there were glaring errors in the text due to misinformation, the book continues to be one of the major classics on the subject on Santería.

The Julian Press's hardcover edition of the book was so elegant that within months of its publication there were several major publishers interested in the paperback rights. And ironically enough, the first publisher to whom I submitted the manuscript and who turned it down, was the one who bought the paperback rights. That publisher was Doubleday and the paperback division was Anchor. Two years after *Santería: African Magic in Latin America* was published by Julian Press in Hardcover, Doubleday published it in paperback. Close to ten years later, Original Publications bought the publishing rights to the book. They have been publishing it successfully ever since.

All that of course is ancient history and the main reason for writing this preface is to explain to the reader why this new edition of the book is being published. But a history of this book would be incomplete without this small but necessary tribute to the man who made it possible.

Santería: African Magic in Latin America was my first book. I wrote it because I felt that its subject matter was fascinating enough to warrant, not only one but many books to be written about it. Since that first effort, I have written five other titles about Santería, and several other writers, many of them very gifted, have also contributed to the literature on the subject. It continues to be my hope that academic and public interest on Santería will not wane, and that many more researchers will devote their talents to the study of this intriguing religion.

When I first wrote about Santería, my knowledge of the religion was sketchy at best. I had not undergone any of the major initiations and my information came from second-hand sources. The santeros I interviewed in the course of my research were wary and distrustful. Many lied and gave incomplete and often false answers to my questions. At the time Santería was a completely closed religion, and only those who received initiations were allowed to enter into its mysteries. There was no information available, and even Lydia Cabrera's marvelous classic *El Monte*, gave no clue to the in-depth secrets of Santería. There was plenty of folklore available, tales and anecdotes, but very little solid information on the actual practices of the santeros. One of the santeras I interviewed at the time, who later became a good friend, still laughs at all the inaccurate data and often blatant lies she told me during those early conversations. Why did she do it? To protect her religion. She knew I intended to write a book and she had no intention of divulging any secrets to me or to anyone who was not a practitioner of Santería.

It was not until I had received several of the basic initiations of Santería, such as the Necklaces, Elegguá and the Warriors and the Cofá of Orunla, that the santeros finally relented and opened up to me. I had succeeded in proving to them that I was not interested in exploiting their religion but rather experience it and present it to the world as a powerful new religious system.

The misinformation that I received during my early study of Santería, and which formed an intrinsic part of *Santería: African Magic in Latin America*, is the reason why this new edition is being published. I have carefully edited the book, excised all the wrong information and added the pertinent, now correct data. This editing work was long overdue and I have wanted to do it for years. Original Publications, aware of the need to present a corrected text of the book to the public, had agreed to do a new edition. Nothing has been changed from the original text except the inaccuracies. I hope you enjoy reading the book every bit as much as I enjoyed writing it and rereading it again. It was like coming back to an old friend, staunch and true. It's my favorite among all my books. I hope it becomes one of your favorites also.

Migene González-Wippler
Spring, 1992
New York City

Introduction

Latin American magic, better known in Spanish as *Santería*, had its birth in Nigeria, along the banks of the Niger River. This is the country of origin of the Yoruba people, who, among many other African tribes, where brought to the New World by slave traders over four centuries ago. The Yorubas brought with them the colorful mythology of their religion, known in Cuba as *lucumí* and in Brazil as *macumba*.

The Yoruba people originate from Southwestern Nigeria. They constitute a large number of ethnic groups, such as the Egba, the Ketu, the Ijebu, and the Ife, among others. At one time they had a powerful and complex social structure that was organized in a series of kingdoms, the most important of which was that of Benin. The kingdom of Benin lasted from the twelfth century until 1896, when it was dispersed by the English colonists. Benin was a form of theocratic autocracy, where the *oba*, or king, had absolute power. The advanced culture of the Benin civilization can be appreciated in the beautiful works in bronze and ivory, dating from archaic times to the seventeenth century, that can be found in many museums throughout the world. In the beginning of the seventeenth century, the Ewe people invaded the region of Dahomey and the neighboring kingdoms, forcing the Yoruba tribes to migrate to the Nigerian coast, where many of them were captured by the slave traders and brought to the New World.

The most important and interesting aspect of the Yoruba

culture is their mythology and religious practices. Extensive studies and researches have been made about the Yoruba cult. These studies have shown that the Yoruba pantheon is extremely complex and sophisticated, and strongly reminiscent of the ancient Greeks. Their gods and goddesses, known as *orishas*, are believable and extraordinarily human in their behavior. The term orisha is of uncertain origin. Some anthropologists believe it is derived from the word *asha*, meaning religious ceremony. Others claim it is formed of the roots *ri* ("to see") and *sha* ("to choose"). There are many orishas in the pantheon. Some authorities say that in Africa their number exceeds six hundred. In Latin American only a few of these are known and paid homage to.

As the various African families were scattered throughout the New World by the slave trade, their religious practices were influenced by their new surroundings and the strange languages spoken in the lands of their exile. Each tribe borrowed freely from the customs, the ideas, and the religious beliefs of its adopted land. This brought great diversity into the magic ceremonies of the black man. The rites varied with each tribe. In Haiti, the voodoo cult was propagated by the Nagos, the Ibos, the Aradas, the Dahomeans, and other tribes. In the Spanish and Portuguese colonies, especially Cuba and Brazil, similar magic rites were transmitted by the Yoruba and the Bantu people. Although some of the rituals and ceremonies of Santería are not unlike Haitian voodoo rites, the divergencies are marked. For not only were different tribes involved in the two movements, but also Haiti was under French influence during the slave trade, while other Caribbean countries, such as Cuba, Puerto Rico, and the Dominican Republic, were under Spanish rule.

In Cuba, where Santería has developed extensively, the Yorubas became known as lucumí. This term is derived from the Yoruba word *akumí*, which is the name given to a native of Aku, a region of Nigeria where many Yorubas came from. The Cuban lucumís were deeply influenced by the Catholic iconolatry of their Spanish masters. In their confused imagery, they identified their gods and goddesses with the saints of the Catholic faith. This was the beginning of Santería, which is a term derived from the Spanish word *santo* ("saint"), and literally means the worship of saints. Santería is a typical case of syncretism, that is, the spontaneous, popular combination or reconciliation of different religious beliefs. This syncretism can be appreciated in the fact that most of the Yoruba gods have been identified with the images of Catholic saints.

To the Catholic worshipper, the image of a saint is the ideological representation of a spiritual entity who lived at one time upon the earth as a human being. To the *santero*, or practitioner of Santería, the Catholic image is the embodiment of a Yoruba god.

Santería is a curious mixture of the magic rites of the Yorubas and the traditions of the Catholic church. All the legends and the historical arguments that surround the lives of Jesus, Mary, and the Catholic saints are of great importance to the santero, as these data serve to delineate the personalities of the saints, making it easier to identify them with the appropriate Yoruba gods. But although the santero often finds his way to the Catholic church for an occasional mass, his sporadic visits are sometimes prompted by ulterior motives; namely, he may need some holy water for a spell, or a piece of the consecrated host, or maybe some candle wax with which to harm an enemy. For, in spite of the influence of the Catholic church, Santería is mostly primitive magic, and its roots are deeply buried in the heart of Africa, the ancestral home of the Yoruba people.

Magic has been defined as "any of the arts of producing marvelous effects by means of supernatural powers." Sorcery, on the other hand, implies a form of magic in which spells are cast or charms are used, "usually for a harmful or sinister purpose." This latter definition is not entirely accurate. A sorcerer's aim does not necessarily have to be destructive in principle. Perhaps one of the most accurate descriptions of a sorcerer that I have found is that used by Carlos Castaneda in his book, *A Separate Reality*. In the words of Don Juan, Castaneda's Indian teacher, a sorcerer is "a man of knowledge

and power." Sorcery is "to apply one's will to the *key joint*."
Sorcery is interference. A sorcerer searches and finds the *key
joint* of anything he wants to affect and then he applies his will
to it." Very often, in order to cast his spells and to stress his
dominion over the phenomenal world, Don Juan, as a sorcerer
and "man of knowledge," has recourse to the aid of any of a
number of "allies," whom he "manipulates" at will. These
allies range from hallucinogenic drugs to elemental spirits and
are simply tools used by the sorcerer to accomplish his will. Don
Juan does not label sorcery as black or white, positive or
negative. Furthermore, he tells Castaneda that the "allies are
neither good nor evil, but are put to use by the sorcerers for
whatever purpose they see fit." According to this concept, a
sorcerer is a man of great knowledge and power who can effect
changes in his environment at will, either on his own or with the
help of supernatural entities. This does not preclude the
possibility of the use of sorcery for evil purposes. It is rather
a broad hint to the effect that the actual choice of good or evil
rests with the individual sorcerer. This definition of a sorcerer
is a very accurate description of the work and aptitudes of the
santero, who is a "man of knowledge and power," whose allies
are the orishas of the Yoruba pantheon, syncretized as Catholic
saints.

The magical feats of the santero include helping his consult-
ants get rid of negative influences, cure illnesses, secure
employment, attract a lover or a spouse, improve financial
conditions, and subdue and often destroy rivals and enemies.
Like Don Juan, the santero does not think of his magic as good
or evil. He simply uses it to accomplish his will, and to his mind,
the "ends justify the means." The santero, however, is a
sorcerer whose work is mostly directed to ameliorate or solve
those human problems that seem unsolvable by ordinary means.
Thus he could be classified as a good, or white, magician; but
even then, only because he so chooses. And we must keep in
mind that very often a santero will attempt magical works that
could hardly be classified as constructive, such as the times
when he uses his magical knowledge to punish or otherwise

harm an enemy. For magic cannot be easily classified as good or evil. It is essentially a neutral force, an ability to alter natural laws that is part of the magician's mental and spiritual makeup, and that can be used indiscriminately for destructive or constructive purposes.

Rather than embarking on a lengthy discussion of the ethical aspects of magic, it would seem more interesting to look into the nature of evil for the purpose of attaining a clearer understanding of its intrinsic mechanism.

There are two forms of evil. Negative evil and positive evil. Negative evil is the "polarizing opposite of Good." For example, it is difficult to walk on a slippery surface, because it offers no resistance. There has to be something for the foot to push against to give the body the necessary momentum to take a step. Negative evil is the principle of resistance, of inertia, that enables good to manifest itself. This principle of resistance is the "negative" aspect of negative evil. Its "positive" aspect is the principle of destruction, which is also known by its esoteric name of the "Scavenger of the Gods." According to well-known occultist Dion Fortune, the function of the principle of destruction is "to clear up behind the advancing tide of evolution, removing that which has become effete so that it may not choke or clog evolving life." This explains why God "tolerates" the devil. For the devil is nothing more than the "cosmic thrustblock" of the Deity. Thus it is obviously a necessary evil, a reaction based on cosmic laws, not a chaotic or anarchical force.

Positive evil, on the other hand, has, as its negative aspect, pure chaos, unformed substance, and imbalance. It is the antithesis of order and harmony. It is all that is unnatural and in direct opposition to the creative principle of the universe. It is the absolute denial of the cosmic laws of stability and coherence. The positive aspect of positive evil is the demonic entities that symbolize all the evil imaginings of man that are not compensated by the surplus of good and harmonious thoughts in other members of the same group soul. From these chaotic intelligences flow all the destructive impulses that tempt and

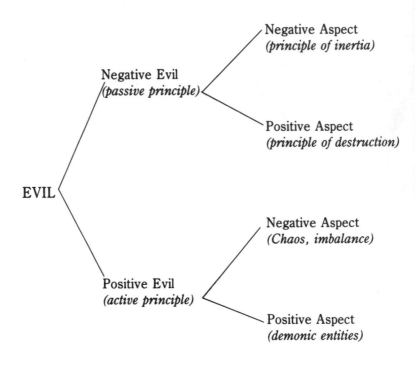

Evil is composed of two polarizing aspects — negative evil and positive evil. Of the two aspects, positive evil is the active-male principle, and therefore the most malefic of the two. It generates and engenders further evil. That which is positive evil is more actively destructive.

corrupt mankind. They probably originated through the practice of black magic across the ages. The black magicians organized and shaped the original evil substances into plastic molds with definite characteristics and personalities. The beings thus created assumed an independent existence and rapidly developed and multiplied their kind. They often become visually perceptible during dreams and hallucinations, and may be tapped and made to manifest themselves physically by means of invocations and conjurations. Very often, certain spells and incantations become charged with great vibratory impulses through repetitive use, and act as keys that unlock the subconscious trapdoors behind which lurk all kinds of cosmic horrors. Once unleashed, these fearful nihilistic entities must be promptly channeled by the black magician and used to accomplish his nefarious purposes — for should he tarry, or be unsure of his next move, these same hellish forces would utterly destroy him. Therefore successful practitioners of black magic are perforce high adepts, with a vast knowledge of natural and cosmic laws. They have to be, in order to survive their constant flirtations with spiritual disintegration.

The santeros do not make use of chaotic forces in their magical work. Their allies, the Yoruba gods, are direct manifestations of the Creative Principle and thus are spirits of light. When he does magical work of an apparent destructive quality, the santero is using the negative aspect of a positive force. For example, when he seeks revenge upon an enemy, he may be using the devastating forces of Oggún, god of war, or Changó, god of fire, to correct an injustice or to "right a wrong." In Order to avoid becoming the eventual recipient of cosmic reprisal for a work of destruction, the santero is careful to state that he has been the victim of the evil machinations of his enemy, and therefore he is entitled to "divine justice." Thus he is able to carry on all the negative aspects of his magical works under the protective aegis of the cosmic laws.

There is another sect in the Caribbean, known as the Congos or Bantus, who work often with evil forces. Their beliefs and practices will be discussed in some detail in this book, as I feel that their work is of interest to both anthropologists and psychologists. The practice of Congo magic has been divided into various branches, the most popular of which is that of *palo mayombe*. The practitioners of this cult are known as *mayomberos* and can be faithfully equated with the proverbial witch doctors of African lore. Magic to them is just a means of survival in a hostile environment that threatens to obliterate their existence at every step of the way. The idea of cosmic retribution does not worry the mayombero. He believes he can escape divine punishment by the proper use of his magical powers, and by "paying" for the "services" of the entities he uses in his spells and ceremonies. This payment consists of food, liquor, a few copper coins, and animal sacrifices.

Understandably, none of the forces used by the mayombero have been syncretized as Catholic saints in the Yoruba tradition. Nevertheless, it is interesting to note that the mayomberos have considerable respect for the alleged powers of the Yoruba deities, and very few of them would dare to enter into an actual confrontation with one of the orishas. it is almost like the proverbial dread of the sons of darkness for the forces of light. This reluctant deference on the part of the mayomberos toward the orishas is not really surprising if one considers their great fame and popularity in Latin America.

Not all the Yoruba deities represented by Catholic saints have the same degree of popularity. Some saints are more popular than others. Their popularity is influenced by their powers and the length of their list of miracles. The saints are known both by their Catholic names and their Yoruba appellations. Very often, a female saint is known in the African pantheon as a male god. A typical case is that of Saint Barbara, who is known in Santería as Changó, the lucumí god of fire, thunder, and lightning. As Changó, Saint Barbara is conceived as a gigantic black man of strong, handsome features and an infectious smile.

The Yoruba deities are earthy and colorful, full of passions and ardent likes and dislikes. They have been thoroughly humanized across the centuries and are believed to descend to earth and take possession of their devotees, who are known as their "children." The possession of a believer by an orisha is an amazing sight upon which many psychological studies have been made. The possessed individual takes on all the supernatural characteristics of the orisha by whom he is believed to be possessed. Under this influence he may collapse on the floor, twitching and shaking, or he may start a violent ritualistic dance that lasts for hours without any indication of physical exhaustion on the part of the person possessed. Most often, however, the person eats and drinks lustily and performs outstanding feats of physical strength and power. Under this influence he is also able to divine the future with stunning accuracy.

It is surprising how strongly Santería has influenced the inhabitants of the Latin American countries. The primitive beliefs and customs, with their barbarous words of evocation, have even found their way to the busy, sophisticated streets of New York and Miami, where Santería flourishes now as powerfully as in the Caribbean islands.

Contrary to popular belief, Santería is not confined to the ignorant and the uneducated. Some of the most devoted followers of the cult are people with extensive educational and cultural backgrounds. The thing that the ignorant and the educated have in common in Santería is the deep conviction that it really works. It is simply magic, both black and white, and it works. Its power is real and vivid. At least they believe it is.

Quite a few of the dictatorships in Latin America have been credited to magic. Many Cubans believe that Fidel Castro, for one, owes his success and his power to the black magic of the Cuban *mayomberos* ("witches"). It is rumored that the powers that placed him in his fortified bastion are African deities. Whether or not this is true, it is unlikely we shall ever find out.

The strength of Santería, therefore, lies in the belief of its followers in the supernatural powers of their gods. In this book, I will discuss in detail the mythology, the beliefs, and the practices of Santería. It is the first time a book has been written about the religion in the English language. I hope it will not be the last. It is a fascinating subject, worthy of serious study.

1
What Is Santería?

When the Yorubas identified their gods with the saints of the Catholic faith, the saints became invested with the same supernatural powers of the African deities. They were invoked by the Yoruba priests to undertake cures, cast spells, and do the same type of magic usually ascribed to the orishas. Each god-saint was credited with certain specific attributes and was believed to control some aspects of human life. All natural phenomena and the common occurrences of everyday living were under the direct influence of the deities.

No one really knows when a culture starts to leave its imprint on another — or how. Throughout the centuries, the Spanish and Portuguese settlers and their descendants became increasingly interested in the ritualistic magic of the Yorubas. The initial interest may have started by a babalawo being able to cure an illness that an accredited physician was unable to conquer — or maybe by the accuracy of the witch doctor's predictions and spell casting. Whatever the reason, the white man began to attend the primitive rites of the African slaves, and occasionally to take part in them. By the end of the nineteenth century, the Yoruba cult had gained many devotees among the Spanish people in the Caribbean areas, notably Cuba, Puerto Rico, and the Dominican Republic, although the latter was also deeply influenced by the voodoo cult. Brazil was also greatly permeated by the Yoruba religion and it is today one of the South American countries where the Yoruba rites are more actively practiced.

As the magical rites of the Yorubas became more popular, the white man, slowly overcoming the natural reticence of the African priests, managed to learn most of their intricate legends and rites, until he was finally allowed to participate in the initiation ceremonies. As soon as he reached adepthood, he rebaptized the practices and named them Santería, that is, worship of saints. He himself became known as a *santero*, or practitioner of Santería. He kept most of the African names of the orishas and the most important rituals, particularly the ceremony of initiation, which he renamed *asiento*, a Spanish word that means seat. The choice of this word may be explained by the fact that the saints are believed to take possession of their initiates and literally "mount" them. The santero is known commonly as the "horse" of the saints. During the initiation the "seat" of the saints, that is, the mind of the initiate (*yaguó*) is conditioned for its future work. A santero is initiated in the mysteries and rites of the orisha he recognizes as his "father" or "mother." The asiento is also known as *hacer el santo*, which means literally "to make the saint." The initiation ceremony will be discussed in greater detail in another chapter.

The modern santero practices very nearly the same type of primitive magic as the old Yoruba priests. He is a zealous guardian of the Africa traditions and is usually notoriously uncommunicative about his beliefs and practices. Since some of his magic would be hard to explain to an *aleyo* ("nonbeliever"), this reticence is not difficult to understand.

In Cuba, the ancient traditions were transmitted orally by the old priests to their descendants and followers in special meetings known as *cabildos*. During the course of these meetings the santeros established the laws and practices of their religion, and made them known to the new initiates. The Yoruba god who was to rule the following year was also determined during the cabildos. Still another method of transmitting the legends and practices of the cult was by means of handwritten notebooks known as *libretas*. Although the cabildos are no longer celebrated, the custom of keeping a written record of the spells and ritual ceremonies of Santería is still observed. Every santero has a *libreta* where he has meticulously written down all the teachings of his sponsor. This custom is very similar to the practice among European witches to keep a book of spells and rituals that is known as the "Book of Shadows."

The basic difference between the African priests and the santero is that the latter practices his magic in the asphalt jungles of big cities instead of in the African wilderness. Santería is simply jungle magic adapted to city living. Its ritual practices are based on sympathetic magic. That is, they are natural magic based on the laws of similarity and contact.

The law of similarity may be expressed by the magical principle that says that "like produces like." On the other hand, the law of contact says that "things which have been in contact with each other continue to affect each other long after the physical contact has been broken." When the type of magic used hinges on the law of similarity, it is known as homeopathic magic. In this system the magician believes he can create virtually any kind of natural phenomenon by acting it out beforehand, often by using natural objects that are in sympathetic alliance with the purpose of the ceremony. The most familiar example of this type of magic is that of a wax doll that is molded in the image of the person to be affected. The magician believes that whatever happens to the doll will also happen to the intended victim. Another example of homeopathic magic, fairly common in Caribbean witchcraft, makes use of a small stone that may be found in a park or an ordinary garden. The stone is picked up and named after the person one desires to influence. The stone is then brought into one's house and thrown on the floor by the door. It is then kicked lightly throughout the house until it rolls under one's bed. As the stone rolls, one should stress that it is not a stone that is being kicked but the person one wishes to dominate. From these two simple examples it is easy to understand the basic principles behind imitative or homeopathic magic.

Contagious magic assumes that things that have been in contact with each other are always in contact. It is thus possible to exert influence on a person if one can only procure something that has been in contact with that person. It may be a piece of clothing or some hair or nail parings. Any of these materials can be used to bewitch their owner in a very real and effective way. For example, hair strands from the victim can be knotted together with hair from the person casting the spell in the form of a bracelet. This bracelet is then work on the right wrist during nine days, all the while willing the victim to come to the magician and bend to his or her desires. Nail parings can be used in perfumes, and clothing can be craftily employed in making rag dolls that represent the victim.

All forms of sympathetic magic assume that things act on each other at a distance through an unidentified and unexplainable attraction, the initial contact being sparked by the will of the magician. This belief in the sympathetic influence exerted on each other by objects or individuals separated by a distance is of tremendous importance in Santería, and indeed in any form of natural magic.

The English magician Aleister Crowley defined magic as the ability to effect changes in consciousness in accordance with the will of the magician. This definition agrees with the magical principles of Santería. But it is not enough to have a strong will to bring about the reaction desired. One must also have faith — the burning conviction that the magic will work. Whether this faith transcends human consciousness and stems from nonhuman entities or whether it is rooted in an unshakable self-assurance is immaterial. What matters is its influence and the sometimes incredible phenomena it can create. In Santería this faith is firmly placed on the mighty powers of the Yoruba gods. The supernatural powers of the saints, in close alliance with the sympathetic magic of the santeros, and their strong determination to succeed, bring about the changes in consciousness described by Aleister Crowley. Naturally the gods do not grant their favors without a suitable offer. This may range from a nine-day candle in the color favored by the god, a dish of honey or of candies, to a basket of fresh fruits or an animal sacrifice. The offer varies with the personality of the god invoked and the magnitude of the favor asked. After asking the help of a particular saint in a given spell, the santero proceeds with the actual ceremony, which he dedicates to the saint, very often reinforcing the spell with an image of the orisha and special prayers. Spells requiring the help of a saint must employ materials that are attributes of that particular orisha. For example, a spell for love enlisting the aid of Oshún would be worked with seashells, beads, honey, animal sacrafice, or pumpkins — all attributes of the goddess. Any candle burned in her name would have to be yellow, which is her favorite color. Table 1 lists some of the most important attributes of the more popular saints.

TABLE 1

Orisha	Colors	Human aspect controlled	Weapon or symbol
Obatalá	white	peace, purity	all white substances
Elegguá	red/black	messages, opens and	a cement head ornamented with seashells
Orúnla	green/yellow	divination	Table of Ifá
Changó	red/white	passion, enemies	double-edged ax, sword, cup, castle, thunder
Ochosi	lavender	hunting, jails	bow and arrow
Oggún	green/black	war, employment	iron, knives, steel weapons
Babalú-Ayé	purple	illness	crutches
Yemayá	blue/white	maternity, womanhood	seashells, canoe, fans
Oshún	yellow/white	love, marriage, gold	mirror, fans, seashells, pumpkins
Oyá	wine	death, cemeteries	fire, thunderbolt

This list is only a partial one. Some orishas, like Oshún and Yemayá, have dozens of attributes and symbols, many of which they share with each other. A complete list of attributes of all the orishas would consume many pages. The best person to judge which orisha should be used on any given problem, and which ceremony would apply best, would be a competent santero. Although some situations fall clearly under the jurisdiction of one of the orishas, there are problems that may necessitate the help of more than one saint. In extremely difficult cases there may be a need to invoke the help of the Seven African Powers, a powerful combination that includes Obatalá, Elegguá, Orúnla, Changó, Oggún, Yemayá, and Oshún.

Images of the Saints

Very often, in order to cast a spell successfully, the image of the orisha being invoked is necessary. As there are very few images of the gods in their African aspects, the santero uses those representing the Catholic personality of the orisha. Some of the images are statues exquisitely made, imported from Spain or Italy, and therefore very expensive. The sizes vary from one to five feet. There are also small plastic statuettes, some of which are manufactured with magnetized bases to be fastened to the dashboards of cars. The cheaper images are paper or cardboard drawings of the saints. The loveliest statue I have seen of any of the orishas is an image of Saint Barbara (Changó) that belongs to my brother, who is very devoted to the saint. Usually Saint Barbara is represented as a girl in her teens, crowned, wearing a white tunic and a red mantle bordered with gold, obviously a royal figure. In her right hand she holds a goblet symbolizing the Holy Grail while with her left she brandishes a sword. The crown, cup, and sword are golden. At her feet stands a small tower, shaped like a fortress. The legend says Saint Barbara lived in the fourth century. Although her life is shrouded in many contradictory legends, most historical sources agree that she was a princess and a Christian. Her father had her imprisoned in a tower because of her beliefs and of her refusal to marry according to his wishes. One tempestuous night he went up to her tower and renewed his demands that she marry one of his chieftains. The insistence with which she clung to her beliefs, and her refusal to do his will, filled him with such fury he drew out his sword and beheaded her. At that precise moment he was struck down by a bolt of lightning, thus creating the legend that gives Saint Barbara power over lightning and fire. The analogies between the virgin martyr and the Yoruba god of thunder and lightning are so marked there is no doubt in the santero's mind that they are both the same. The statue of Saint Barbara that I mentioned earlier is a good example of this identification. The image is about four feet tall, with an exquisite face and a nubile figure, the tunic and mantle engraved with gold leaf, her crown, sword, and cup made of twenty-four-carat gold. Nothing could be more delicate and fragile than this ethereal maidenly figure. Yet the offers at her feet are a glass of rum and a thick cigar, given to the saint in her Yoruba aspect of Changó.

Beliefs of Santería

Santería teaches that every person is assigned, upon his or her birth, a protective guide that is one of the orishas. This guide is known as the guardian angel. Besides his guide the new baby is also assigned a special plant, a birthstone, and an animal. If he discovers the identities of these divine mascots upon growing up, and keeps them with him always, he will be successful and powerful all his life.

The lucky stone of an individual does not have to be a precious gem. It may be a simple colored pebble that he found on the beach and that attracted his attention for no special reason. The unexplainable urge to pick up a stone that is found by pure chance is an indication that the spiritual guide wants you to take it and keep it as a good-luck charm. Naturally, not all the stones found by chance may be considered lucky pieces. The santeros refer to a particular eye-catching stone that makes you feel you just must have it. That stone is probably loaded with good vibrations for you personally, and you should pick it up and carry it with you always. Of course, there are guides who prefer precious stones. Changó, for instance, whose color is red, is partial to rubies, although he will settle for a garnet, a carnelian, or any pretty, bright red stone. Oshún likes the topaz, whose yellow color is reminiscent of the gold of which she is so passionately fond.

It is not true, say the santeros, that a person's birth date has a relationship to his birthstone. In Santería a person's birthday has no spiritual significance. To the santero, the undisputed proof of this fact is that hundreds of thousands of persons are born on the same day, yet they all lead entirely different lives.

The animals that are believed to be beneficent are the goat, the elephant, and the turtle. It is not necessary to keep one of these animals in the house in its living form, thankfully. It is sufficient to have a small image in metal or plastic to receive its benefic influence. On the other hand, the animals that are considered spiritually noxious are all manner of reptiles and venomous insects, such as scorpions and centipedes, some varieties of frogs, all birds of prey, the rat, the crocodile, the lizard, and the spider.

The santeros also believe that water has great spiritual strength as a defensive measure. They recommend to their followers that they keep a small receptacle full of water with camphor under their beds to cleanse away all evil influences. They believe the dark spirits that descend upon us from their vitiated spheres are dissolved in water like sugar or salt. The waters must be changed every week. Preferably they should be thrown out of the house when no one is looking, but under no circumstances should they be allowed to fall on the floor or on the kitchen sink.

Other effective agents against evil entities are garlic and brown sugar. The santeros burn the sugar and the garlic skins in a small pan on a bed of hot coals, and the thick, dense fumes resulting therefrom are allowed to fill the entire house, especially inside closets and in the corners, where the evil spirits are believed to hide. These fumes are known as *sahumerio*. Many santeros also keep a black rag doll in their houses to dispel evil influences.

Although the Yoruba deities understand "every language in the world," there are certain sounds that make them "more propitious and sympathetic.'' For that reason, many of the words used to invoke an orisha are in the Yoruba language. Some of the most common words used in the religion are given in the following list:

orisha any of the Yoruba deities
yaguó initiate into the cult
yubbona the sponsor of the yaguó
aleyo or **aberínkula** a non initiate
araba or **iroko** the sacred tree of Santería. It is known in Spanish as **ceiba**, and botanically, as the five-leaved silk-cotton tree.
iyalocha female practitioner of Santería
babalawo high priest of the religion
agogó or **acheré** an instrument used, together with drums, to call an orisha to the earth.
omo-orisha a santero consecrated to a specific orisha.
oru series of invocations or calls
batá the three drums used to call the gods together with the agogó. They are named Iyá, Itótele, and Okónkolo. The sound of Okónkolo never varies. It is a base upon which Iyá and Itólele speak to each other.
otán special stone sacred to an orisha, and by means of which the god communicates with the santero. The otanes are usually kept in ornamental bowls in the altars of the orishas.
güemilere sacred ceremony of Santería
ileocha temple where the ceremonies are held
eyá a room inside the ileocha
igbodu sanctuary where the talismans and stones of the orishas are kept
ibán-balo backyard of the temple
akoñrin singer or caller of the orishas
okoni teacher
akoyú wise man
bámbula dance
agbebé fan used to help cool the orishas when they become very heated or upset. It is a symbol of Yemayá and Oshún

amalá   food offered to Changó
foribale   genuflexion made in front of the drums or the
   sanctuary
moddu pué   thank you
aché   grace, power
Iré   good luck
owó   money
ilé   house

Herbal Lore

The basis of the major spells of Santería are herbs, plants, roots, and flowers. Every santero is a competent herbalist who can cure practically every disease with an herbal brew, or cast a tremendous spell with a few flowers. Every plant is believed to have a spiritual entity that guards it. All herbs are believed to be alive, full of ache (''power''). Each root, flower, tree, or plant belongs to one or the other of the orishas, whose permission must be asked whenever the plant is used. Most herbs have a dual purpose, for cures and for magic. Garlic, for example, is used in teas to lower high blood pressure and also to dispel evil influences. *Artemisa* is used in teas against appendicitis and also in purifying baths. *Anamú (petiveria alliacea)* is used as an abortive and also to dispel trouble and dissension. The coconut has extensive uses; the water is often used as a diuretic and the meat is used in divination.

Some herbs are considered evil and are used only for works of destruction. A typical example is poison ivy (*guao*). According to the santeros this plant belongs to the devil. They believe that if a person touches the guao and suffers the typical violent rash for which the plant is famous, he should hit the leaves with a wooden stick, spit on the roots, and insult it with the vilest language. If he does this he will develop an immunity against the plant that will never dare to injure him again. The guao is used to create trouble by the mayombero, who mixes it with pepper, bones from the heads of a black cat and a black dog, a tarantula, salt, sulfur, and graveyard dust. The mixture is then placed near the house of the intended victim, who shortly thereafter will meet with all sorts of trouble.

Another plant that is greatly used by the santeros is a bush known as *escoba amarga (partenium hysterophorus)*, which is used in purifying baths and to drive away the *abikús*. An *abikú* is a mischievous spirit that reincarnates in a human child who dies in early childhood. There is a belief among the old santeros that the only way to drive away the abikú is to beat it with a branch of the escoba amarga. Whenever a child is very sickly and cries constantly, his body is believed to be inhabited by an abikú, and he is lightly thrashed with the branch, usually on Wednesdays. Modern Santería tends to scoff at these beliefs, but there are still some people who call on the santero whenever a child believed to be an abikú dies young. The santero makes a mark on the body, as they believe that the abikú will return to plague the family again. When another child is born in the same family, his body is inspected to see if it has the same mark that was placed on the dead child. If such a mark is found, and according to the santeros it often is, the santero is promptly summoned to "tie" the new born to the earth so that he will not die also. This is accomplished by securing to the child's ankle or wrist a small chain that must not be removed until he is past the puberty age.

The basis of the rituals and ceremonies of Santería is to be found in the legends of the Yoruba gods. The origins of the orishas and their syncretism with the Catholic saints are of great importance if one wishes to understand the personalities of the gods and the principles of Santería.

2
The Legend

In the beginning, according to Yoruba myth, there was only Olodumare — a being, without definition because his essence cannot be comprehended by mortal men. Olodumare is composed of three separate and equally undefinable spirits: Olodumare Nzame, Olofi, and Babe Nkwa.

Olodumare Nzame is the creative principle. He created heaven and earth, the sun, the moon, the stars, and all plant and animal life on this planet. After he finished his work of creation, he asked his two companions if they liked what he had done. Both agreed that Olodumare Nzame had accomplished great and marvelous things, but pointed out the need for the creation of an intelligent being to rule over the earth. At their suggestion, Olodumare Nzame created the first man from the mud, in their own image, giving him intelligence, beauty, and immortality. This first being was named Omo Oba, and soon became so conceited with his great beauty and power that Olodumare, in a fit of anger, ordered Nzalam, the lightning bolt, to destroy all life upon the earth. Unfortunately, Olodumare had created Omo Oba immortal, and therefore Nzalam could not kill him. Omo ran away and hid himself in the bowels of the earth, where he is surrounded by the fire and brimstone caused by Nzalam's scourge. He changed his name to Olosi and comes periodically to the surface of the earth to incite men to break Olodumare's laws. Some time after this unfortunate incident, Olodumare felt sorry at the sad state of the earth, which had become dry and blackened as a result of Nzalam's fire. All the three spirits that form the deity descended upon the planet and mercifully covered it with new life. They created a new man to rule over the earth, but did not give him the gift of immortality. This being is the major Yoruba deity, Obatalá.

After this second creation, Olofi, one of the aspects of Olodumare, was put in charge of the earth's affairs, and the other two spirits. Olodumare Nzame and Baba Nkwa, left the planet to continue their work of creation elsewhere in the universe. Olofi, therefore, is the aspect of the deity that is conceived by the Yorubas as man's personal God.

One of the first things that Olofi did to ensure that men on earth would not follow Olosi's example, and eventually destroy themselves, was to give Obatalá eleven commandments. They were

1. You will not steal.
2. You will not kill, except in self-defense and for you sustenance
3. You will not eat human flesh
4. You will live in peace among yourselves
5. You will not covet your neighbor's properties
6. You will not curse my name
7. You will honor your father and mother
8. You will not ask more than I can give you and you will be content with your fate.
9. You will neither fear death nor take your own life
10. You will teach my commandments to your children
11. You will respect and obey my laws

According to one legend, Olofi gave Obatalá a wife whom he named Yemmu. Obatalá is represented as a man on horseback, dressed in white, holding a lance in his hand. His color is white and all the articles devoted to him are also of this color. Yemmu is represented as a black woman, sitting down while breastfeeding an infant. But this legend is often contradicted by some santeros who have their own explanations and legends to explain the origins of the orishas.

Of the union of Obatalá and Yemmu were born a son, Aganyú, and a daughter, Yemayá. Aganyú is the god of the volcanoes. Yemayá is the Yoruba moon goddess and controls the waters. She is represented as a beautiful woman with yellowish skin, dressed in white and adorned with blue beads.

According to the legend, Aganyú and his sister Yemayá were married and had a son, Orungán, who was so handsome and talented that his father became ill with envy and finally died. When Orungán became a man, he fell in love with his mother and forced her into an incestuous relationship. The goddess, consumed with grief, cursed her son, who soon died. She then climbed to the top of a high mountain where she died of sorrow. Her abdomen burst upon her death and she gave post-humous birth to fourteen of the gods of the Yoruba pantheon, conceived from her union with Orungán. As her abdomen burst, the waters flowing from within her body caused the universal deluge. From Yemayá's bones were born Obafulom and Iyáa, the Adam and Eve of the Yoruba myth. The place where the goddess died became known as the holy city of Ile Ife, where Obafulom and Iyáa lived and propagated the human race.

The fourteen gods that were born of Yemayá were:

Changó God of fire, thunder, and lightning. He is one of the major deities of the pantheon and is identified by many as Takata, the god of stones. Changó lives in the clouds in a shining castle, whence he sends his thunderbolts whenever he has been offended. He is very feared and respected and has a large following in Santería.

Oba Goddess of the Oba river and the acknowledged wife of Changó. Like her, her cult originated in the land of Takúa. She is very jealous of her handsome and philandering husband and constantly follows him around.

Oyá Goddess of the Niger river and the favorite concubine of Changó. She is sometimes represented with nine heads, which is the number of tributaries of the Niger river. Her messenger is the wind, Alefi. She is the patroness of justice and helps to improve memory. She holds a flame in her right hand and it is from her that Changó gets his power over fire.

Oshún   Goddess of the Oshún river and also one of Changó's mistresses. She is one of the most popular of the Yoruba deities and is the patroness of rivers. She is the Venus of the Yoruba pantheon and the goddess of love and gold.

Ochosi   God of the hunters and birds and wild animals. His symbol is the bow and arrow.

Olokun   A hermaphrodite god who wears very long hair and who lives in the depths of the ocean floor with a great retinue of mermaids and tritons.

Olosa   The favorite concubine of Olokun. She is a benefic goddess who helps fishermen. Her messenger is the crocodile.

Chankpana   God of smallpox. He is represented by an old man nursing a lacerated leg. The flies and mosquitoes are his messengers. His symbol is a red and white cane. He is often identified with Babalú-Ayé, the patron of the sick, who is also represented as an infirm old man.

Dada   God of unborn children and of gardens. He is represented by a pumpkin embellished with seashells.

Ayé-Shaluga   God of fortune and good luck. He is represented by a large seashell.

Oke   God of the mountains and protector of those who live in high places.

Orun   God of the sun. He has very few followers.

Ochu   At one time goddess of the moon. Like Orun, she is no longer very popular.

From various other sources, the Yoruba added to their list of gods the following deities:

Aroni   God of medicine.

Ayé or **Ayá**   Midget goddess of the jungle.

Oyé   Giant god of storms.

Ochumare   Goddess of the rainbow.

Olimerin   Monstrous deity with four heads and goat's feet. He is the protector of villages.

Chiyidi God of nightmares. He is an evil entity who is used to torment enemies.

Olarosa Protector of homes. He is represented by an old man walking with a cane across the portal of a house.

Osachin Patron of doctors. He is represented as a bird of prey perched on the branch of a tree.

Oggún God of war and iron. His origin is obscure. Some legends say that he was also conceived of the union of Obatalá and Yemmu. He eats dogs and is the patron of ironworkers. Before going to war, the Yorubas used to sacrifice to him a human victim or a black dog. He is one of the most popular gods of the cult.

Ibeyi Twin gods who protect infants. They are represented by two small children.

Elegguá One of the most powerful gods of the cult. He opens and closes all doors. His image is always kept on the floor, behind a door, as he protects the entrances to all the homes where he is kept. He is generally represented as a head made of clay or sandstone, with the eyes and the mouth formed with seashells.

Orúnla Owner of the legendary Table of Ifá, the divination system used by the babalawos and by means of which one can see the past and the future as in a mirror. He is also known as **Ifá**, god of impossible things and of palm trees. He was the first owner of the Table of Ifá. He is the god of fertility and gives his help to all women who desire to have children.

The Syncretic Mixture

All the Yoruba deities that became part of the cult of Santería were identified with Catholic images. The most important ones are enumerated in the following list:

Yoruba god	Catholic saint
Olorún-Olofi	Crucified Christ
Obatalá	Our Lady of Mercy (Las Mercedes)
Oddudúa	Saint Claire
Aganyú	Saint Christopher
Yemayá	Our Lady of Regla
Changó	Saint Barbara
Oyá	Our Lady of La Candelaria
Oshún	Our Lady of La Caridad del Cobre
Ochosi	Saint Isidor
Dada	Our Lady of Mount Carmel
Ochumare	Our Lady of Hope
Oggún	Saint Peter
Babalú-Ayé	Saint Lazarus
Ibeyi	Saint Cosme and Damian
Elegguá	Saint Anthony
Orúnla	Saint Francis of Assissi

According to this syncretic mixture, Our Lady of Mercy married Saint Claire and from their union were born Saint Christopher and Our Lady of Regla. The brother and sister were married. Out of the incestuous relationship between Our Lady of Regla and Saint Christopher were born Saint Barbara, Our Lady of La Candelaria, Saint Isidor, Our Lady of Mount Carmel, and Our Lady of La Caridad del Cobre, among others.

Incest and Reincarnation

The incestuous and often outrageous behavior of their gods does not seem to trouble the santeros. No one would dare to condemn a deity for his or her quasi-human frailties. To do so would entail a punishment far too terrible to chance it. Neither does the stunning fact that some of the orishas change sex in the syncretic mixture bother the santeros. Since Santería is inter-mixed with spiritualistic beliefs, they explain the change by arguing that their gods existed before all other beings, and that after their mythical deaths they returned to the earth reincarnated in new bodies. The idea of reincarnation is an intrinsic part of Santería. For the santero, the boundarie between the world of spirit and that of men is very fine indeed. During the course of their captivity the Yorubas started to recognize their gods behind the white facade of the Catholic images. It was like assisting at a costume party and finding there a group of very close and dear friends. The myths were revived, the cult started anew, and with the influence of the new images, Santería was born.

Black Magic

The Yoruba pantheon does not have many intrinsically evil beings. Iku is the spirit of death. What is termed black magic or witchcraft in the Caribbean and South America is not part of the Yoruba tradition. It is a practice linked essentially to another tribe: the Bantus, better known in the Caribbean as Congos. Their magic is known as *palo monte or palo mayombe.*

3
Rituals and
Ceremonies of Santería

The most important religious ritual of the cult is the asiento, the "making of the saint." But before one may take part in this formal initiation ceremony, it is necessary to undergo various preliminary rites.

Necklaces — Collares

The first step toward becoming a santero is to acquire the protective bead necklaces of the cult (*elekes*). They are known as *collares* and are specially made for the neophyte by his madrina or padrino ("sponsor"). Before the madrina prepares the necklaces, she must ascertain by means of the seashells which saint is the guardian angel of the aspirant. Initially, there are five necklaces, one for each of the following orishas: Obatalá, Elegguá, Oshún, Yemayá, and Changó. Later on, if he so desires, the neophyte may acquire other necklaces, such as those of Oggún, Oyá, Babalú-Ayé and Aganyú. The necklaces are believed to protect their wearer against all evil as long as they are being worn. While he is wearing the necklaces the neophyte may carry on his normal everyday routine, but he is not to bathe or to undertake any form of sexual activity. If he wants to take a bath or have sexual intercourse, he must remove the necklaces and put them back on when he is finished.

The colors of the necklaces vary according to the orishas to which they are consecrated. Following is a list of the various elekes and the traditional colors in which they are made.

Obatalá all white beads
Yemayá seven white beads alternating with seven blue beads
Oshún all yellow beads; also five amber beads alternating with
    five red beads
Changó six white beads alternating with six red beads
Eleggua three red beads alternating with three black beads
Oggún seven green beads alternating with seven black beads
Oyá brown beads striped blue
Babalú-Ayé all white beads striped blue
Orúnla a green bead alternating with a yellow bead
Aganyú blue and brown beads

Before he prepares each necklace the santero invokes the proper orisha in the Yoruba language, asking the god to bless the eleke. The beads must always be strung with a cotton thread, as the latter must soak up the liquid of a special *omiero* in which the necklaces are kept during seven days after they are finished.

When the elekes are ready they are washed in a river, and an offer of a chicken and some honey is made to Oshún by the riverside. Back in his house, the santero prepares an omiero with the herbs ascribed to the patron saints of the necklaces. He sacrifices the necessary animals to the gods and makes a suitable offer of fruits and candies. The necklaces are placed in the omiero and seven days later they are presented to the aspirant in a complicated ceremony that lasts several hours. The initiate must dress in white during and after the ceremony. The clothes must be new.

The Making of Eleggua

After receiving the necklaces, the next initiation to be undertaken is that of Eleggua and the Warriors. The Warriors include Oggún, Ochosi and Osun, which is said to foretell when danger is near. As the making of Eleggua will be discussed at some length in Chapter 6, I will confine myself here to the preliminaries and the purposes of this ceremony.

As I have already mentioned, Eleggua is the messenger of the orishas, the one who opens and closes all doors. His help and goodwill are essential to the santero. Should Elegguá be unpropitious, all the magical practices of the santero would come to nothing. During this second visit the padrino or madrina looks again at the seashells, but this time the purpose is to learn as much as possible about the past, present and future of the consultant. All this information must be included among the ingredients that will be used in making Elegguá. Also during this registro the santero finds out which of the 21 paths of Elegguá is the one that pertains to the consultant. This information is also important because it tells the santero exactly how this particular Elegguá must be prepared. This initiation is usually given by men. If a woman is the one giving it, then she must ask a male priest to prepare Elegguá for her, as this orisha has certain secrets that only a man can provide.

The preparation of Elegguá is time consuming and delicate. The final product could hardly be called a work of art, all the materials shaped into an almost amorphous mass vaguely resembling a human head. The sizes of the Elegguás vary from a few inches to over a foot tall. The eyes, ears, and mouth are shaped with tiny seashells, while the nose is formed of the same material as the rest of the head, usually cement. This deceptive simplicity of the orisha's image is an effective camouflage of its tremendous powers: for the massive head that the santero places in the hands of his disciple is not merely a representation of Elegguá, but the god himself. The neophyte receives Elegguá made in relation to himself. The making of Elegguá is one of the deepest mysteries in Santería. Both santeros and babalawos are empowered to give the initiation of Elegguá and the Warriors, although the babalawos will dispute this point and claim that they are the only ones who can do it correctly.

At the same time he receives Elegguá, the neophyte also receives the cauldron of Oggún with all the war implements of the god and of the two other warrior saints, Ochosi and Osun. These are known as the Warriors in Santería, as together they fight to protect the initiate.

The reason why the cauldron is given to the novice at this time is that Elegguá, Oggún, Ochosi, and Osun are considered to be the warriors of the Yoruba pantheon, and they always "walk together." Oggún and Ochosi have already been mentioned but Osun has not. He is one of the more obscure orishas and is usually represented by a small cup surmounted by a tiny rooster. The cup is generally kept by the santeros near their front door, ensuring that it is always higher than the head of its owner. Should the cup fall down without being touched, it is announcing grave danger for its owner, who should immediately consult his padrino or madrina to avert the evil foretold.

The head of Elegguá is also kept near the front door, on the floor, or as near the floor as possible. Some practitioners of Santería keep Elegguá in a small cabinet or inside a closet. He must be near the door because he guards it at all times.

The symbolic meaning of the acquisition of the necklaces and of Elegguá is analogous to the military tactics of attack and defense. While the necklaces provide protection against all forms of evil and enemies, Elegguá and the other warrior orishas make it possible to attack and overcome enemies with impunity. These are "the foundations" of Santería, and whoever "owns" them is armed to the teeth while sheathed in impenetrable armor.

Making the Saint

The initiation ceremony of Santería, known as asiento or "making the saint," is a very expensive affair, often costing many thousands of dollars. The reason for this high cost is that there are many expensive items needed for the ceremony, such as sheep, goats, and many other animals that are sacrificed to the orishas during the ceremony.

Before the asiento takes place, the novice undergoes a thorough ritualistic cleansing of the head, known as *rogación de cabeza*. This is a comparatively simple ritual during which the madrina annoints the head of the initiate with a paste made of ground coconut meat, cocoa butter, powdered eggshell (*cascar-*

illa), and other ingredients. She invokes the Guardian Angel of the novice to purify him and keep him from all evil. The paste must remain for some time on the novice's head, usually overnight. It is then removed and the asiento takes place.

The main purpose of the initiation ceremony is to condition the mind of the novice to act as a receiver and transmitter for the saints, particularly the orisha who acts as his guardian angel. For this reason all the emphasis of the asiento is placed on the initiate's head.

All initiations are not the same. They vary according to the saint who is being invoked to take possession of the yaguó or initiate. An asiento celebrated to bring down a female orisha would differ vastly from one held to invoke one of the warrior gods. The main difference would be in the animal offers. While the standard practice is to sacrifice sheep, goats, hens, roosters, and pigeons to most of the saints, a female orisha like Yemayá would also require ducks among the offerings. Changó, on the other hand, would want turtle, and the warrior gods, Ochosi, Elegguá, and Oggún, would need no less than three possums.

The identity of the god to be ''crowned'' on the yaguó's head must be ascertained by a babalawo or an oriate before the asiento ceremony. It is vital that the saint invoked to take possession of the initiate is the same one who acts as his guardian angel. If the wrong saint is ''brought down,'' utter chaos would ensue, causing the true guardian angel to withdraw his protection from the yaguó and kindling the wrath of the orisha invoked by mistake. Both orishas would direct their fearsome anger at the unfortunate yaguó, who would then require countless cleansings and special prayers to rid himself of the resulting avalanche of troubles and ill luck that would start to plague him.

The asiento can be attended only by the initiate, his sponsor, the babalawo, whose duty it is to sacrifice the animals, and other santeros. Only those who have already ''made the saint'' can be present at the ceremony. The asiento takes place in an *igbodu* or sanctuary. The yaguó's head is shaved entirely and a series of concentric circles are drawn on his scalp with natural dyes in red, white, blue, and yellow. The hair that is shaved and the remnants of the dyes are kept by the madrina, as they must be buried with the santero when he dies. The initiate is dressed in colorful robes, of the color attributed to his orisha on the third day after the ceremony. The highlight of the asiento is the *parada*, when the yaguó collapses on the floor, possessed by his orisha, who is invoked with the batá. While the yaguó is in this trance, he receives the ache, which is the blessing of the saint, in the form of a cross made on his tongue with the flat surface of a razor blade. Immediately afterwards, the madrina or yubbona places in the mouth of the initiate three grains of pepper, some honey, and a bit of smoked possum (*jutía*). The madrina then tears off the head of a chicken and offers its warm blood to the yaguó, who drinks it thirstily. When the initiate awakens from this trance he sits on a throne that is erected for him on a corner of the igbodu. He sits there majestically surveying the ritual sacrifices of all the animals, and drinks a little of the blood of all the decapitated heads as they are offered to him by the yubbona.

The yaguó must pay his madrina a certain amount of money for the asiento. This money is sacred and is called the *derecho*. The derecho is first wrapped in a large leaf and then in a piece of cloth of the color sacred to the yaguó's orisha. The money thus wrapped is covered by a small carpet upon which is placed the throne of the yaguó.

After the ceremony is over, the yaguó remains in the igbodu seven days, accompanied by the yubbona, who deeds him only certain foods during this time. He is also washed every day with a special liquid called *omiero*, which is prepared with the juices of twenty-one herbs sacred to all the orishas, mixed with some of the blood of the animals sacrificed during the asiento. The yaguó drinks some of the omiero every morning during these seven days. After the week is over, he returns to his house and in another ritual called dodobale, he pays homage to the batá. Three months after the asiento, a special ceremony is conducted to cleanse the yaguó from any lurking impurities. At this time, the yaguó is declared a full-fledged santero and is able to practice, and take part in, all the magical rituals of Santería. From his madrina he receives the *otanes* of his saint, which are several stones of various shapes and sizes believed to be inhabited by the orishas, and to which are ascribed all the supernatural powers of the saints. The otanes are kept in special bowls (*soperas*) of the colors favored by the orishas. To pray in front of the soperas where the otanes are kept is the same as invoking the orishas to whom the stones are dedicated. The belief in the otanes is traced to a Yoruba legend. Whenever a just man died, according to the myth, Olofi rewarded his good deeds by turning his soul into rain. This rainwater, which was the good man's soul, would then fall on a river near the place where the man had lived. Shortly thereafter, the rainwater would be turned into a stone. A certain time after the man's death, several members of his family would consult a babalawo and ascertain where the man's soul was "residing." They knew it would be in a stone near their house because Olofi always rewarded good people in this manner. With the babalawo's help they soon located the stone, which was then brought to the house and placed in a special bowl of the color favored by the dead person. After some time, people started asking the spirits who resided in the otanes to help them in their human problems. The spirits complied and the practice grew to include the Yoruba deities among the spirits inhabiting the stones. This is the origin of the belief in the otanes as habitations of the gods.

At the time he receives the otanes and the soperas, the initiate is also given the weapons or working implements of the orishas and the seashells (*caracoles*) that belong to that particular orisha. The seashells are part of a set of eighteen, known in Santería as the Diloggun. The santeros consider the seashells the most precious of their possessions and guard them literally with their lives. A santera I know keeps her set in the bank, where she considers them far safer than at home. To lose the shells would be a major catastrophe for the santero, as that is how he can communicate directly with each orisha. The seashells are said to be the mouthpieces of the saints.

After he receives the asiento, the santero must study with an *italero* who will teach the santero how to read and interpret the seashells. The italero is an experienced santero who has made a lifelong study of the Diloggun. He is the only one who knows how to interpret the oracle accurately. The seashells are the means by which the saints speak to the santero. The Diloggun must be read on a small carpet (*estera*) and is interpreted according to the position in which the shells fall.

During the asiento, the new santero also wins the right to work with five of the orishas, besides his own guardian angel. The five saints are usually Obatalá, Elegguá, Changó, Yemayá, and Oshún. If the yaguó's guardian angel happens to be one of these five orishas, another saint is substituted for it.

The Diloggun — Los Caracoles

The seashells (*los caracoles*) are, as I have already mentioned, the most important divination procedure in Santería. Although the Diloggun is composed of eighteen seashells, only sixteen are used by the italero in interpreting the oracle. The seashells can be bought in any botanica, and are often acquired with smooth and unbroken shells. Each smooth shell is filed until its two serrated sides are exposed. The underside of the shell is naturally hollowed, while the top side vaguely resembles a tiny mouth with a minuscule set of pointed teeth. The latter is the side used in reading the Diloggun.

During a registro with the Diloggun, the santero, or italero, after special invocations to the orishas, holds the sixteen shells in both hands, rubs them together, and throws them on the straw mat (*estera*). He repeats this action several times, interpreting each pattern of seashells according to the position in which they fall. Each pattern is known as an oddun, and has a name and a number assigned to it. The shells are read according to how many of them fall with their top side uppermost. If only one seashell shows its top side, it is said to be the first "letter" of the Diloggun and the first offun. Each letter or pattern "speaks" for one or several of the orishas, and is interpreted according to the legend or proverb that is traditionally associated with it. The proverbs or legends are applied to the particular problem faced by the querent, and based upon the circumstances of each individual case, the italero gives his interpretation of the oracle.

The Diloggun is very similar to the ancient Chinese system of divination known as the I Ching, which uses a number of sticks that are thrown on a table and interpreted according to the positions in which they fall. As in the Diloggun, the I Ching uses proverbs to render judgment on the situation faced by the querent.

The first twelve patterns of the Diloggun and their respective names, as well as an abridged version of the proverbs, are given in the following list. The colorful legends associated with the odduns are too lengthy, and regrettably cannot be cited here.*

Oddun #1 *Name: Ocana Sode. Speaking:* Elegguá Changó, Aganyú, Obatalá, and the dead
    Proverb: "The world was started by one."
Oddun #2 *Name: Ellioco. Speaking:* The Ibeyi, Ochosi, Elegguá, Oggún, Obatalá, and Changó
    Proverb: "There is an arrow between brothers."
Oddun #3 *Name: Oggúnda. Speaking:* Oggún, Oshosi, Obatalá, Olofi
    Proverb: "Arguments and tragedy are caused by misunderstanding."
Oddun #4 *Name: Ellorozun. Speaking*: Yemayá, Oshún, Aganyú, Olofi, Oyá
    Proverb: "No one knows what lies at the bottom of the sea."
Oddun #5 *Name: Oche. Speaking*: Olofi, Oshún, Orúnla, Elegguá
    Proverb: "Blood that flows through the veins."
Oddun #6 *Name: Obbara. Speaking:* Changó Oshún, Elegguá
    Proverb: "A noble king does not tell lies."

---

*For the complete history of the seashells and detailed instructions on how to interpret the Diloggun, the reader is directed to the book on the subject by the author, entitled *Introduction to Seashells Divination.*

Oddun #7 *Name: Oddi. Speaking*: Elegguá, Yemayá, Oshún, Oggún, Obba, Orúnla
  Proverb: "Where the hole was dug the first time."
Oddun #8 *Name: Elleunle. Speaking*: Obatalá and all the saints
  Proverb: "The head carries the body."
Oddun #9 *Name: Osa. Speaking*: Oyá, Obatalá, Oggún, Obba, Llansa
  Proverb: "Your best friend is your worst enemy."
Oddun #10 *Name: Ofun. Speaking:* Obatalá, Oshún, Oyá
  Proverb: "Where the curse originated."
Oddun #11 *Name: Ojuani. Speaking*: Elegguá, Babalú-Ayé, Osain, Nana Buruku (the moon), Obba
  Proverb: "Be distrustful; carry water in a straw basket."
Oddun #12 *Name: Ellila. Speaking*: Changó, Oyá, Yewa
  Proverb: "You are defeated through your own fault."

Invocations to the Orishas

It is a tradition among the santeros to "speak" to the gods in the Yoruba language. This custom is derived from the belief that words are sources of energy and that the energy accumulates with the repetitive use of certain phrases.

The power of the spoken word has been traditionally associated with the world's major religions, particularly Catholicism and Judaism. Everyone is familiar with the use (now abolished) of Latin formulas in Catholic liturgical ceremonies. In the Jewish doctrine the twenty-two letters of the Hebrew alphabet have great symbolical significance, each letter having a numerical value as well as a special meaning. The first letter, aleph, for instance, has the numerical value of one, and signifies an ox. The most powerful combinations of Hebrew letters are those that make up the names of God and the angelic forces. The spiritual and magical power of these words is believed to be so great that the vocalizing of them can set in motion gigantic vibratory impulses throughout the entire universe, creating vast changes in the structure of the order of things. These changes can be either beneficent or destructive depending on the names invoked and the purpose of the invocation. The

Tetragrammaton, the four consonants of the Hebrew name for God, are considered too sacred and powerful to be pronounced by the ordinary man. The word Adonai ("Lord") is substituted for the name. The transliteration of the four consonants is given as JHVH, IHVH, JHWH, YHVH, or YHWH. Because the Hebrew language does not have any vowels, it is a matter of speculation how the four consonants were pronounced in ancient times. The vowels of Adonai or Elohim are inserted in many Hebrew texts so that modern reconstructions are YAHWEH or JEHOVAH, but Hebrew scholars agree that these are incorrect interpretations of the holy name. The correct pronunciation was so jealously guarded among the priesthood that it eventually became lost for future generations.

In the first chapter of Genesis, God says: "Let there be light." And at his spoken command, light is created. Thus from ancient times to the present, words are power. This is also evident in Santería. The babalawo must know the Yoruba language and the ritual invocations to the gods. Following are some of the traditional invocations of the most popular of the orishas.

Elegguá

IBARAKOU MOLLUMBA ELEGGUÁ IBACO MOYUMBA IBACO MOYUMBA. OMOTE CONICU IBACOO OMOTE AKO MOLLUMBRA ELEGGUÁ KULONA. IBARAKOU MOLLUMBA OMOLE KO IBARAKOU MOLLUMBA OMOLE KO. IBARAKOU MOLLUMBA AKO ELEGGUÁ KULONA ACHE IBAKOU MOLLUMBA. ACHE ELEGGUÁ KULONA IBARAKOU MOLLUMBRA OMOLE KO AKO ACHE. ARONGO LARO AKONGO LAROLLE ELEGGUÁ KULONA A LAROLLE COMA. KOMIO AKONKO LARO AKONKO LAROLLE ELEGGUÁ COMA KOMIO ACHE. AKONKA LARO AKONKO LARO AKO ACHE IBA LA GUANA ELEGGUÁ. LAROLLE AKONKO E LAROLLE E LAROLLE AKONKO AKONKO LAROLLE AKONKO LAROLLE AKONKO LA GUANA E LAROLLE.

Changó

CHANGÓ MAINI COTE CHANGÓ MANI COTE OLLE MASA CHANGÓ MANI COTE
OLLE MASA CHANGÓ ARA BARI COTE CHANGÓ ARABARICOTE ODE MATA ICOTE
ALAMA SOICOTE YE ADA MANICOTE ADA MANICOTE ARAN BANSONI CHANGÓ MANI
COTE CHANGÓ MANI COTE ELLE MASA CHANGÓ ARAMBSONI CHANGÓ ARA
BARICOTE ODEMATA ICOTE SONI SORI CHANGÓ ARABARICOTE ARABARICOTE ARA
SORI HE HE LELE AGUO GUE GUE ARO A MAYO GUERA HE HE GUE GUE HA MAYO
AMAYO GUERA OKOLOTE ARO EGUE ARO AMAYO GUERA MANICOTE CHANGÓ
MANICOTE OYE MATE MANICOTE OYE MATA ALABAO CHANGÓ ARABARICOTE
CHANGÓ ARABARICOTE ALAGUAO BARICOTE OYE MATA ARABARICOTE SORI ACHE
CHANGÓ MANI COTE SOICOTE ARA ADOMEMATA ODE ODE ODEMATA ODE ODE
OYE. MATA ARA BARICOTE SORI SORI SORI ODE MATA ODE MATA SORI ACHE
BARICOTE ARA BARICOTE SORI ACHE CHANGÓ.

Obatalá

GUALLE GUALLE LO MIO GUALLE GUALLE LO MIO GUALLE GUALLE LO MIO
GUALLE PARA META GUALLE. PARA META ARE GUALLE GUALLE LO MIO GUALLE
GUALLE LO MIO GUALLE GUALLE LO MIO GUALLE PARA META GUALLE PARA META
AREKU BABA ARA BABA ARE BABA ARE LLE BARA KUERURO OPIYO LA LLELLEO
OKU YI BANDELEO BABA ARE ALLE BABA ARE ALLE BABA KUE URO OMI LIÑO BABA
KUE URO OMI LI ÑO OCUNI BANDELEO OBATALÁ EKUE CHORO ICHOLU ICHOLO
HE HE OBATALÁ IFA IFA LLUMILA ILLA PILOSO IFA IFA LLUMILA ILLA PILOSO ILLA
KUKE KUKE OMO KU ARO OBA OBA PELLE TOMA OBATALÁ ALLE ALALLEE BABA
ARA LLE BABA KUE URO OMI LI ÑO OCUNI BANDELEO BABA KUE URO OMI LI ÑO
GUAYE GUAYE LOMIO GUAYE GUAYE LOMIO PARA ME KE GUAYE GUAYE LO MIO
PARA MEKE GUAYA PARA ME KAO GUAYE LO MIO ARE GUAYE PARA METAO GUAYE
PARA MEKE GUAYE PARA META.

Oggún

AGUANILLEO OGGÚN ARIBO AGUANILLEO OGGÚN ARIBO EGUN EKO
MARE HO MORIRE EGUN EKOMARE HO MORIRE ARERE AGUERE ARIBO OMO
RIRE OGUNDE BAMBA AGUANILLE OGGÚN ARIBO AGUANILLEO OGGÚN
ARIBO EGUN EKO MARE HO MORIRE EGUN EKOMARE HO MORIRE ARERE

HE ARIBO LLANYA OGGÚN ARERERE AREREO HE ARIBO LLANYA HE ARIBO
LLANYA OGGÚN ARERE AREREO HE ARIBO LLANYA AGUANILLEO ARERE
ARERO AGUANILLEO OCHE OGUÑA ARERE HOE HOE ARIGOÑAÑA ACHE
OGUÑA ARERE O HE ARIGOÑAÑA ACHE ARERE HOE ARIGOÑAÑA OGUNDA

Yemayá

SOSIRIBAOE ILLALE YABUMBAO LLALE IMILATE ALLAVA OMIO EKO ILLALE
YAMUBAO LLALE OMILATE ALLAVA OMIO AGUAREKE AGUAKUELONA HE YEMAYÁ
AGUAREKE AGUAKUELONA HE YEMAYÁ AGUAGUELONA HE AGUAREKE ASTARAFIO
OLOCUM DALE COLLUMLLA HA MI PA OMIO EKO LLALE YA LLUMBAO LLALE
OMILATE ALLAVA OMIO YEMAYÁ AO OLOCUM ABOKO MI YEMAYÁ YEMAYÁ HO
OLOCUN ABOKO YEMAYÁ TIRAZECUM TIRALECUM TIRALECUM ABO YEMAYÁ
YEMAYÁ LORDE ABOKO HAE HE LLALORDE LLALORDE HE YEMAYÁ LORDE ABOKO
HAE ABOKO LARIOTE LARI OTE OTE OTE YEMAYÁ LORDE LARI OTE LARI OTE
LARIO LARIO LARI OTE LARI OTE OTE OTE LARIO LARIO OTE.

Oshún

ILLA MI ILE ORO ILLA MI ILE ORO VIRA YE YEYE OYO YA MALA YE ICU OCHE
OCHE OYE OGUA ITA LOCUM OCHA DEGUALLO ORO MAMA KEÑA ORO MAMA KEÑA
LLAMA AQUI ICU OSHÚN ILOCO ODDE ILA IKA TOLOYE ILLARDE APETESI OLORO
OLORO TU OLORO OPAO OLLENA ANDE HA LA MOLO RIFA IMBE IMBE MA YEYE
IMBE IMBE LORDE IMBE IMBE MA YEYE IMBE IMBE LORO IMBE IMBE MA YEYE
IMBE IMBE LORDE IMBE IMBE MA YEYE IMBE IMBE LORDE IMBE IMBE MA YEYE
IMBE IMBE LORDE IMBE IMBE MA YEYE IMBE IMBE LORDE IMBE IMBE LAYEYE
IMBE IMBE LORO VIA YE OYO YA MAL YE ICU OCHE OCHE OGUA ITA LOCUM OCHA
DEGUALLO A MAORIFA IMBE IMBE LORO.

Santos Lavados

Very often there are practitioners and believers in the
religion who want to be able to work with a certain saint, but do
not want to undergo the long and costly ceremony of initiation.
In such cases they must participate in a simpler ritual known as
santo lavado, in which they receive some of the secrets of the

saint but not all of his or her powers. This ceremony is very similar to the asiento, but the head is not shaved and the saint is not invoked to possess the believer.

It is also a very common practice in Santería for a practitioner or a sympathizer of the religion to receive only the necklaces and the Elegguá without any further rituals.

The Babalawo

The babalawo is diviner, witch doctor, and father confessor all rolled into one. Not all the santeros are babalawos. Only those who are the children of Orúnla, the owner of the Table of Ifá, can rightfully aspire to the high office of the babalawo. Also, only men can claim the title. The reason for this apparent discrimination against women is that Orúnla, who is the patron of the babalawos, is a male orisha and his priests are always men. The Table of Ifá is only used during initiations or complex situations. It is of vital importance in determining a person's guardian angel or ruling orisha.

The most important duty of the babalawo, besides the interpretation of the Table of Ifá, is the sacrifice of animals during the major ceremonies of the religion.

The powers of the babalawo are limitless and his word a law in itself. Whenever a member of the religion (and often a noninitiate) has a problem, he brings it to the babalawo who analyzes it by means of the okuelé, a long metal chain interspersed with eight pieces of coconut rinds, shaped like medallions, This is the babalawo's most common divination system. The Table of Ifá is a wooden tray with African carvings upon which a special powder called *yefá* is spread. The babalawo makes lines with his finger on the powder to produce certain patterns which he then interprets as the voice of Orúnla. The round tray, known as *Opon Ifá*, is believed to represent the cosmos.

This self-styled specialist is also a competent herbalist and unlicensed physician. He cures all kinds of diseases, and very often in Santería, the members of the religion prefer the home remedies of the babalawo to the prescribed medicines of a regular doctor. They insist the babalawo knows more about the powers of herbs than any modern doctor. After all, most drugs are processed from plants anyway. So why pay a high price for a fancy bottle to a fancy medicine man, when the same remedy, maybe even a better one, can be found at the house of the babalawo for a fraction of the cost.

Perhaps one of the most common complaints brought to the babalawo are marital and love problems. At these he is also a specialist. After one look at the problem, he promptly prescribes the remedy needed, which may range from special flower baths to more complicated ceremonies.

The power of the babalawo rests upon his reputation for accurate divinations and skillful advice. The greater his acumen, the greater his clientele. One of the most regular prescriptions of the babalawo or the santero is a good luck talisman known as *resguardo*, which is a Spanish word that means "protector." As the name indicates, the function of the resguardo is to protect its user at all times. A typical resguardo is prepared by an *iyalocha* of my acquaintance, using Changó as the guardian spirit of the resguardo. She makes a small bag of red velvet and fills it with certain herbs, aloes, brown sugar, spices, and other ingredients and closes the bag, stitching it with red thread. She then attaches to the bag a small gold sword with the name of Saint Barbara inscribed upon it, and invokes Changó to protect the owner of the resguardo from all evil. Invariably, whenever danger threatens the user of the resguardo, the sword breaks and must be immediately replaced. According to this santera, her resguardos have become so popular that she prepares dozens of them every week. A woman who purchased one of these talismans told the santera that the small sword broke within hours after she got it. A few days later she declined an invitation to go dancing with some friends and thus escaped serious injury when their car skidded and crashed into a tree. The santera replaced the broken sword and told the woman to thank Changó for her narrow escape.

Some of the remedies prescribed by the santeros and

babalawos require very strong stomachs. A particularly shock-
ing love spell is reputed to be quite infallible and is highly
recommended by some santeros. The only ingredients required
are a few grains of hard, dry corn. The person casting the spell
must swallow the corn and then wait patiently until the body
disposes of the grains naturally. The corn is then removed from
the feces and washed, toasted, and ground into powder. This
powder is then given to the unsuspecting victim in coffee, wine,
or tea. It is said that the person who drinks this philter will
always remain in the power of the one who gave him the potion.

Death of a Babalawo

The death of a babalawo is often as colorful as his life. The
same day of his death, a group of babalawos meets at his house
to learn what is to be done with the magical implements of the
deceased. This is usually ascertained by means of the Table of
Ifá, with which they question Orúnla, the patron saint of the
babalawo. The ceremonies are lengthy and open only to other
babalawos.

The death of a santero is also surrounded by many rituals and
traditional ceremonies, which can only be attended by initiated
santeros and babalawos. Not even family members of the
deceased are allowed to be present at the ceremonies, if they
are not initiated. Most of the time, the spirit directs the
santeros to bury his working implements with his body. The
otán-orishas, the stones consecrated to the orisha to whom the
santero was dedicated, must be disposed of according to the will
of the deity to whom they were consecrated. Sometimes the
orishas decide the stones should be buried with the santero and
sometimes they decide they should be given to one of the
godchildren of the santero or a member of his family. The body
is dressed in the same vestments the santero wore on the day
of his asiento. The hair that was cut off his head during the ritual
is placed upon the breast of the cadaver. A clay vessel is then
filled with the color dyes used to paint the head of the babalawo
during the asiento, and with other implements that will accom-

pany the body to its final resting place. All the santeros present at the ceremony throw crushed corn silk into the clay vessel, as well as ashes and pieces of dry okra. This means that the babalawo is freed from all his earthly obligations. All the santeros turn their backs to the clay vessel and the *oriate*, or master of ceremonies, kills a black chicken by crushing its head against the floor. The dead bird is also placed inside the vessel. This receptacle is placed by the side of the coffin until just before the burial. It must then be taken to the cemetery before the body leaves the funeral parlor. It is thrown into the open grave toward the place where the body's head will lie. Just before the body leaves for the cemetery, all the santeros sing and dance around the coffin, lead by the oriate, who beats tempo on the floor with a wooded cane embellished with colored ribbons. The goddess Oyá, who is the patroness of cemeteries, descends upon one of her omo-orishas and cleanses the place with her *iruke*. The body is then taken to the cemetery and properly buried. Nine days later, another ceremony takes place to cleanse the spirit of the babalawo with coconut milk. On the first anniversary of the santero's death the last ceremony is celebrated to sever completely his ties with the world of the living. Only then is his soul considered to be at peace. All these ceremonies take place to ensure that the soul of the deceased will not return to earth to plague the living. For very often, a family or an individual is haunted by a spirit that is not able to rest. The santeros believe that the only way to send a recalcitrant spirit away is by means of fire. They prepare a torch with some dried plants and with the flames they fan the air all over the haunted house. The fire is believed to frighten away the spirits, who cannot stand the heat.

On the second of November, the day of the dead, a dish of cornmeal and a glass of water are offered to all the *ikús* ("dead"). Nine candles are also burnt during the next nine days to give light and peace to all the souls in purgatory.

Spiritual Masses

After the death of a santero a spiritual mass is usually celebrated at a gathering of spirits. This spiritual mass follows a Catholic mass, which is said nine days after the santero's death. The spiritual mass consists of flowers and candle offerings to the soul of the departed, which is invoked and asked to renounce all its worldly possessions and to purify itself. A group of mediums sits facing a table laden with flower vases and perfumes, notably Florida water and a heady fragrance known as Lotion of Pompeii. The relatives and close friends of the santero sit by the sides of the table and wait for the spirit of the santero to manifest itself. This does not always happen, but when it does, it is a sure sign that the spirit knows the transition it has undergone and is on its way to a better life.

Some old-timers feel that these spiritual masses are not enough to help the spirit gather strength. They believe it is also necessary to feed the soul by placing some food in a corner of the bathroom or in the courtyard. The offerings to the dead are usually bread, water, cigars, candles and food cooked without salt. The food is left overnight and then it is brought to the woods where it is left for the wild creatures to eat it.

Offers of Animals

As I have already mentioned, Eleggúa is the most feared and respected of all the orishas. He must always be kept happy, for he can ruin the work of all the other orishas if he so chooses. Fortunately, he is very easy to please, because he is a great glutton who thrives on candies and cakes. To keep Eleggúa happy it is usually sufficient to place his image on the floor, behind a door, and to place in front of him a small dish with candies and chocolates. A dried coconut, a cigar, rum and candles are also helpful. The orisha consumes the spiritual essence of the food and the tobacco during the course of one week. At this time, the candies and the tobacco are taken to a park or to the woods where the animals may eat them.

Everything must then be replaced with new offerings. There are times, however, when these simple offers are not enough.

When a person is "crossed," that is, his luck is gone or he is under the influence of a negative spell, Elegguá must come to the rescue. And he will not do it, unless he is "talked into it." The best and most assured way to get Elegguá's help is by making him the offer of a young chicken. This must be undertaken by an experienced santero. First the bird is covered with honey, rum, and lard. The santero then asks the saint if he wants the blood of the chicken. If Elegguá says yes, the santero tears off the head of the chicken and gives *eyé* ("blood") to the oricha. The blood is allowed to drip on top of the gods' image and the floor. It is then wiped off the floor with the chicken feathers.

To be on the receiving end of this type of cleansing is quite and unforgettable experience and one that is likely to reshape the most skeptical mind. I witnessed this ceremony in New York City a few years ago. A friend of mine had told me she knew of a santera who worked wonders and I decided to pay the woman a visit. At the time I was contemplating a trip to Europe and I was curious about the outcome of my traveling plans. The santera consulted Elegguá by means of four pieces of coconut rinds, another divination system that will be discussed in detail in Chapter 5. Elegguá's answer was that I would do better to remain in New York as I would not be able to carry out my plans the way I wanted. Furthermore, the trip posed a very grave danger to my personal safety and the only way I could overcome this threat was through the sacrifices of a chicken and an offer of fresh fruits. I agreed very promptly to bring both offers to the saint as soon as possible, and the very next day I returned to the house of the santera with a young male chicken and a basket full of fresh fruit. The santera conducted the cleansing ceremony, tearing off the head of the chicken in front of Elegguá's image and guiding my hand while I spread the blood over the floor with a handful of feathers. The fruit basket was placed on the *canastillero*, or small cabinet, where the santera kept the saint's image. After the cleansing was over, she used again the coconut rinds to ask Elegguá if he were satisfied with the sacrifice. The orisha expressed his approval of the ceremony and told the santera that I would be protected against physical harm during my traveling but otherwise the trip would be a total disappointment. Undaunted by this prediction, a few days later I left for Europe as scheduled, only to find out that Elegguá's prophecy came true sooner than expected, and I was unable to accomplish anything worthwhile. The second part of the oracle predicting personal danger became evident during a flight between Copenhagen and Frankfurt, when the plane in which I was traveling developed technical difficulties and had to return to Denmark. Already disappointed with my lack of success and badly shaken with the plane incident, I decided to return to New York immediately. The plane in which I made the return flight also developed technical difficulties. It circled the airport for two hours with a faulty landing gear, but it finally landed without any trouble. When I stepped out of the plane, I saw the landing strip was covered with foam and there were fire engines near the landing area, all anticipating a major disaster.

Sometimes a goat or a sheep is sacrificed instead of a chicken. The choice of animal alway rests with the orisha himself. In order to avoid being blamed for sacrificing the animal, the santero or the babalawo are careful to state loudly that it is Oggún who did the killing. Oggún is the patron of iron and steel, the metals used in the making of the sacrificial knife.

Very often an animal is offered to an orisha without killing it. This animal then becomes a sacred object, the exclusive property of the orisha to whom it is dedicated. It must never be killed or harmed in any way unless the saint demands it. These animals are believed to rid the houses of evil influences. To kill one of these animals without the orisha's permission is to incur his anger, which can be a very uncomfortable experience.

Before the santero offers an animal to an orisha, he must find out by means of the seashells or the coconut rinds whether the god accepts the animal, and what is to be done with it. The animals traditionally associated with the most popular gods are as follows:

Obatalá female goat, pigeons
Elegguá chicken, rooster, possum
Changó rooster, sheep, ram, goat
Yemayá duck, turtle, goat
Oshún white hen, female goat, sheep, calf
Oggún the blood and feathers of red or black roosters, all four
legged animals
Orúnla black hens
Oyá preferable hens

The Güemilere or Tambor

The *Güemilere* or the tambor are feasts celebrated in honor of a saint. They are held for various reasons. One of these is to thank an orisha for a particularly big favor. But the most impressive of these *fiestas de santo* are those held on the birthdays of the saints. There are only four orishas whose birth dates are known. They are:

Changó	December 4
Babalú-Ayé	December 17
Obatalá	September 24
Yemayá and Oshún	September 7 and 8

These dates coincide with the birthdays of the corresponding Catholic saints.

The most popular of the tambors are the ones celebrated in honor of Changó. The fiesta usually takes place in an ileocha or in the house of the santero who is honoring the saint. A big buffet is prepared with all the foods preferred by Changó, notably okra, cornmeal, apples, bananas, and all kinds of fruits and cakes. Often served is the traditional drink of Changó, called *cheketé*, which is made with bitter oranges and cornmeal, and sweetened with brown sugar and sugar-cane syrup. Alcoholic beverages are frowned upon by the most conservative santeros. Also no one should smoke during these rituals because Changó tends to eat the burning end of cigars if he takes possession of

1 Changó (god of fire), one of the Yoruba deities. The figurine, reputedly brought to Europe in the 16th century, is carved from wood and styled by the baroque sculptor, Balthazar Permaser. The gem adornments were designed later.

3 (center below) Changó's double-edged sword.

2 A primitive statue of Yemayá.

4 Representation of Yem as a mermaid.

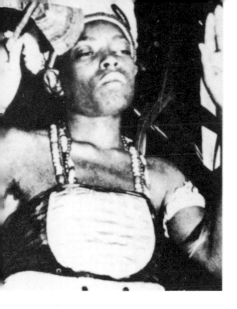

5 (above) An iyalocha possessed by Changó, holding the double-edged ax which is the symbol of the god.

6 (right) The initiate (Yaguó) with his head shaved and painted with vegetable dyes, awaits the ceremony of the asiento.

7 (below) At a güemilere, one of the believers collapses on the floor, at the feet of a possessed omo-orisha.

8 (right) The three drums used in the ritual ceremonies of Santería (batá).

(a)

(b)

(c)

9 (above) The yaguó during the ritual ceremo[ny] of the asiento.

10 (left) (a) Altar of a santero; (b) canastillero where Elegguá's image is ke[pt] (c) the cauldron of Oggún with his implemen[ts]

11 (below) Covered with the blood and feath[ers] of the animal sacrifices, the yaguó collap[ses] during the asiento, possessed by his god.

12 (above) Priests of Obatalá, dressed in white, the color attributed to the god.

13 (right) Animal offerings.

14 (below) The babalawo divines the future with the Table of Ifá.

15 (left) A talisman of Osain.

16 (below) An image of Elegguá
made with sandstone and sea shells.

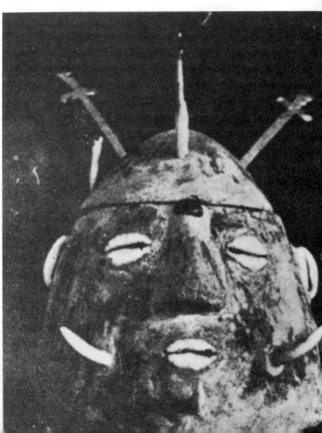

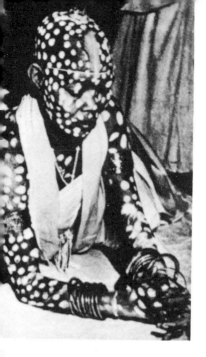

17 (left) A novice of the goddess Oshún.

18 (below) An iyalocha personifying Yemayá-Olokun, dressed in blue satin, a beaded veil over her face, and the sacred fan (agbebé) in her hand.

19 (left) Wearing his necklaces as a stethoscope, a santero in Brazil uses his healing powers to "cure" a believer. The painting on the wall is an artist's rendition of St. Anthony, who is identified by many santeros as Ifá and by others as Elegguá.

20 (below) (a) Talisman of a mayombero; (b) magic nails used to protect the home; (c) vititi mensu, the magic mirror with which he can foretell the future; (d) masango or nkangue, a spell cast to dominate a person.

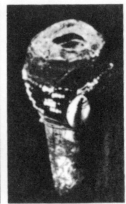

(a)　　　　　　　　(b)　　　　　　　　(c)

(a)

(b)

21 Religious procession in Havana in honor of (a) Yemayá; (b) Oshún; (c) the batá or sacred drums of Santería.

(c)

someone during a tambor.

At the appointed time, the ceremonies begin with the offerings to the dead (the *eggun*). Some food is taken to the backyard or to the bathroom where the dead are believed to eat. (The food of the *eggun* is always cooked without salt.) The dead are also offered fruits, water, coffee and candles. After this offering, the batá drums begin to play invocations to the orishas, starting with Elegguá. These music, where nobody dances, is known as the *Oru* and is always played facing the *plaza* or offerings to the orishas. All the various toureens containing the symbols and implements of the saints surround the offerings. This is known as the throne or *trono*. If the tambor is given to celebrate the initiation of someone into the mysteries of an orisha, the initiate or *yaguó* surveys the dancing and the people, from the middle of the *trono*. Sometimes he sits and other times he stands and sways to the music of the drums. He is splendidly arrayed in satin and damask in the colors of his orisha.

Soon the atmosphere becomes suffused with the heat of sweating bodies. It is usually at this time that the main attraction of the tambor takes place. One or more of Changó's omo-orishas (omo-Changó) become possessed by the thunder god. This is known in Santería as "subirse el santo a su caballo," which means literally, the saint climbs upon his horse. The saint in this case is the omo-Changó.

When a santero becomes possessed by his ruling orisha, he takes upon the characteristics attributed to that deity. A woman possessed by Changó adopts masculine attitudes. The female initiates of the orisha often wear pantaloons under their skirts because when they become possessed by the thunder god they often tear their skirts off or lift them over their heads. This is a typical action of Changó who is very virile and does not like skirts on a body he is occupying however temporarily.

Once Changó has taken possession of a body, he wants to drink and eat all his special foods. After Changó has eaten and drank to his satisfaction, he turns his attention upon the audience, who then ask his advice on their problems, and question him about all their pressing affairs. The behavior of the

omo-orisha tells the experienced santeros whether the possession is real or assumed. Any pretentious make-believe is
ignored contemptuously by the santeros. In Cuba, false possessions were punished with *Oddániko*, a severe beating with a
leather crop. As a result, most possessions were genuine.

The omo-orisha loses all consciousness during a possession,
and his personality disappears, to be replaced by that of the god.
A truly possessed omo-orisha feels no pain and can drink boiling
oil from his cupped hands without burning himself. I have seen
an iyalocha possessed by Changó bang her head against a wall
with such violence that I felt sure she would get a brain
concussion. But she woke up from her possession perfectly
refreshed, without even a shadow of a headache. A possessed
omo-orisha can predict the future with uncanny accuracy and
often describes scenes taking place thousands of miles away as
if he were able to see across time and space. Most of the time
other orishas come to the tambor to help a god or goddess
celebrate their birthday. They all joke and dance together and
have a great time, often at the expense of one of those present
at the güemilere. The omo-orisha seldom has any recollections
of what has transpired in the course of his possession. He
usually complains of feeling light-headed, very thirsty and
hungry afterwards.

At one of these tambors, one of those present at the feast
decided to play a trick on an omo-orisha who was possessed by
Oggún. He crushed some glass and dropped it into the god's
cheketé and then dared the omo-orisha to drink it. Oggún
swallowed the cheketé in one gulp and turning to the prankster
told him that while the body of the omo-orisha would not be
harmed by the crushed glass, the insult to the god's dignity
could only be paid with death. The next day the man who
swallowed the crushed glass woke up in perfect health, while
the one who put the glass into the drink woke up vomiting blood
and died a few days later of an internal hemorrhage.

An orisha does not climb upon his horse exclusively at a
güemilere. He may decide to possess a body whenever he feels
like it. Lydia Cabrera, in her classic work on Santería, "El

Monte'' related the story of a santero devoted to Obatalá, the first deity of the Yoruba pantheon. Every day for a week, the santero of the story asked Obatalá, who is the patron of silver, to give him some money.But somehow, in spite of all his invocations, the money was not forthcoming. Enraged with the orisha's silence, the santero promptly wrapped the god's image in a dirty black rag and hid it in his latrine. I may add at this point that Obatalá is the god of purity and that his color is white. Thus the outrage was doubly injurious. A few days after this incident, the santero became possessed by Obatalá, who took him thus possessed to his nearest neighbor. After arriving at the neighbor's house, the orisha told everyone there that they should tell the santero that he must pay for the outrageous treatment to which he had submitted the orisha by staying indoors during the period of sixteen days, without stepping outside during that time. This did not seem a very had punishment, but the culprit was not repentant of his deed, and after Obatalá left his body and he was given the orisha's message, he shrugged his shoulders and returned home without paying any attention to the god's command. All during the following week, he engaged in every impure act that he knew would offend Obatalá. Within a month of this new rash act, he got into a fight with a street vendor who was accidentally killed in the struggle. After a lengthy trial, he was found guilty of homicide and sentenced to sixteen years in prison. To the other santeros, this was Obatalá's punishment to his omo-orisha for his repeated offenses.

One of the most dangerous orishas to displease is the goddess Oshún. Although she is the goddess of love and usually has a very sweet and amiable disposition, when she becomes offended she is merciless and unforgiving. A santero I know told me that not very long ago he assisted at güemilere in the Manhattan residence of a well-known New York lawyer, in honor of Oshún. It was a great feast and the buffet was a catered affair, full of delicacies, tropical fruits, and exotic dishes. Soon after the ceremony started, the goddess took possession of one of her omo-orishas. She paraded herself among the guests, colorfully wrapped in a yellow silk stole. The fact that the omo-orisha was a man did not deter the goddess from behaving at her most flirtatious. One of the men at the güemilere made an offensive remark in a loud voice, expressing his opinion of the omo-orisha, whom he openly branded as a frustrated transvestite. The goddess did not seem offended at the crude remark. She approached the trouble maker, and pointing at him with a forefinger, she pronounced these cryptic words: "Five *irolé* for you and five *irolé* for my omo-orisha." *Irolé* is a Yoruba word that means day. And indeed, five days later both the offender and the omo-orisha died of the same intestinal disease (the entire abdominal area is sacred to Oshún). Why the unfortunate omo-orisha was punished in this case is a mystery to everyone.

When the santeros want an orisha to leave a body they make the possessed omo-orisha sit down and they cover their head with a white handkerchief. They blow air in his ears and ask the god in the Yoruba language, to leave the body. Then they call the name of the omo-orisha aloud until he answers.

The belief in the possession by orishas is so deeply rooted in Santería that practically every nervous disease, such as epilepsy or hysteria, is attributed to an orisha taking possession of his horse.

After the orishas leave the güemilere, everyone eats and drinks merrily as in any ordinary party. Then the batá pay the final homage to the orishas and the ceremony is over.

4
Magical Practices

The belief in spiritualism for the solution of personal problems is very deeply rooted among Spanish-speaking people. Whenever a person has any serious problem, he ponders the advisability of consulting a santero for the solution. To illustrate this belief I will cite a recent experience of a santera of my acquaintance. She told me that some time ago she went shopping in a department store in El Barrio, the Spanish quarter in New York City. She stopped by the cosmetics counter, trying to decide on a suitable wedding present for a friend. Suddenly she felt the presence of someone behind her. She could sense the person was deeply disturbed about some emotional problem. She turned around slowly and found herself facing a young woman who was staring at the santera with anxious eyes. Unable to control herself, the santera reached out one hand and placed it lightly over the woman's arm. "Don't worry," she said, "I know your problem. It has to do with your husband. If you want I can help you." The woman did not seem surprised by this unorthodox approach from a perfect stranger. Her reaction was just as spontaneous as the santera's. "Yes," she answered, "You are right. My husband has just left me. I need help. What is your advice?" While they stood by the cosmetics counter, the santera pulled out a notebook and a pencil from her handbag and calmly proceeded to write out a list of ingredients for flower baths, *sahumerios*, and a series of herbal aspersions for the house. She also instructed the woman on how to prepare a love perfume and told her what type of prayer to use to bring back her husband. When she finished her instructions she said good-bye to the woman and wished her the best of luck. They never saw each other again. It was simply a spontaneous exchange between a person who needed help and one who had help to give.

Some questions may still lurk in the reader's mind as to what is the purpose of Santería. Why do the santeros worship the saints? What do they expect to gain through their worship? These questions are easily answered if we remember that the santeros believe that every aspect of human life is controlled by an orisha. Thus through the worship of the various saints the santeros believe they can control and rearrange all the natural phenomena around them. They believe they can effect changes in any facet of human experience just by invoking the proper god.

The best way to exemplify the magical practices of Santería is to examine some of the most typical problems brought to the santero.

How the Santero Works

The santero is a consulting expert. His expertise is human life. This may sound rather ambitious, but it does not exceed the santero's claims. He believes he can control life and alter it as he will. He can only do this through his direct links with the saints; therefore, he is always careful to observe all the mandatory rites of the religion and to keep the orishas happy with frequent candle and fruit offerings.

The people who consult the santero do so for a vast variety of reasons. Some are ill or suffering from nervous conditions, others believe they are being attacked psychically by some deadly enemy, still others need help in securing employment or in controlling a wandering spouse or lover. The santero has an answer and a remedy for everyone.

The santero generally uses the seashells during a registro. With the shells or Diloggun he asks his saint-guide to answer any of the questions the inquirer may have and to provide a solution or advice on his immediate problems. After the saint answers, the santero tells his client what the orisha said and what he can expect in the near future. It is at this time that the santero's skills are put to the test. For unless the orisha suggests the actual solution or remedy for a specific problem, the santero has to dig into his bag of tricks and find the remedy himself. This is no mean feat, considering the types of problems that are brought to the santero, but an experienced and capable initiate of Santería can accomplish amazing things.

Let us take a look at some of the dilemmas that have been presented to a santero of my acquaintance and see how this modern Cagliostro used his knowledge of magic to solve them.

Love Magic

Several years ago the santero of our story was consulted by a young woman about a love affair. It seems the girl had just met a very nice and highly eligible young man and was very interested in finding out what were her chances of capturing his interest on a permanent basis. The santero consulted Oshún, the patroness of love and marriage, and learned through her intercession that the young man liked the santero's client but that there were several other girls vying for his attention. This of course called for strong protective measures and the santero was ready with a whole arsenal of magical weapons. The first thing he advised his client was to buy a small image of Oshún in her Catholic aspect of Our Lady of La Caridad del Cobre. The image was to be bought with the intention of always remaining faithful and grateful to Oshún for her help in securing the undivided affections of the man in question. It was to be placed on a small table or shelf in the girl's bedroom. The girl was also instructed to buy a yellow, nine-day candle, of the type that comes encased in glass. She was to ascertain that the candle could be taken out of its glass enclosure, as she was to inscribe her lover's name on the candle five times with her own name written across it, also five times. The candle was then to be dressed with five different types of oil, namely, *sígueme, vente conmigo, yo puedo y tu no, amo*r, and *dominante.* (All these ingredients are readily available at any of the religious goods stores known as *botánicas.*) After the candle was fully anointed it was to be replaced inside the glass. Before the girl could light the candle, however, she had to complete the second part of the spell, which consisted of a small dish of honey at the bottom of which she had previously placed a photograph of her lover. Over the photograph she was to place five small fishing hooks. The allegory was simple. The honey is a symbol of love, of everything that is soft and sweet. It is also one of the main attributes of Oshún. The fishing hooks are also the property of Oshún, who is the patroness of all river waters. With the hooks Oshún would be able to capture the young man and with the honey she would soften him and fill him with great love for her petitioner. The santero cautioned his client to taste some of the honey in the dish before offering it to Oshún. The reason for this precaution was that according to the Yoruba legend one of Oshún's enemies, aware of the orisha's great predilection for honey, tried to poison the saint by introducing some very powerful venom in this substance. Ever since that time Oshún will not accept any offerings of honey unless they are tasted in her presence. After the honey was tested the girl could go ahead and light the candle in Oshún's name, asking the goddess to so inveigle the five senses of the girl's lover that he would think only about her and forget all his other interests for her sake. (The reason for the repetitive use of number five in this spell is that it is the number attributed to Oshún in Santería.) After the candle was lit the girl was not to call or contact her lover in any way, as he would be coming to her before the candle was spent. The santero did not hear from his client for nearly a year after this first consultation and he assumed all was going well with her. He was not far from the truth as he found out during her second visit. This time the girl told her advisor that the spell has worked wonderfully, that her boyfriend loved her madly, that they were very happy, but that in spite of all her promises and complete devotion, she could not get him to marry her. The thought of matrimony was totally alien to his nature and every time she mentioned it he threatened to leave her. What could she do? Much, said the santero. This necessitated Oshún's attention again. Only this time the situation called for more drastic measures. The best ebbó (''spell'') to use would be that of the lily bulb and the man's sperm. As this spell will be described in detail in the Appendix, I will not discuss it here. It is one of the most powerful and best-known spells of Santería. The main ingredient is the onionlike root of the lily, which is hollowed and filled with several oils and other ingredients. Over the oil is affixed a floating wick made of a cotton wad soaked in the sperm of the victim. This original and personalized oil lamp is lit every day for an hour preferably at nine in the evening, making sure that no one knows of its existence. The man who is the subject of this spell is unable to resist it. He must submit himself to the will of whoever is burning the lamp. For, together with the oil, the very essence of his being, in the form of his sperm, is also burning. The santeros believe that a man's sperm is a symbol of his manhood. Whenever his manhood is diminished or affected in any way, his will weakens. At this point he can easily be preyed and prevailed upon without being able to defend himself. By the time he realizes what has happened, it is usually too late to take any preventive measures. The santero's client was elated and full of praise for the santero's powers when her boyfriend, unable to resist such a magical fusillade, surrendered his bastion and acceded to marry her. The santero was pleased that the spell had succeeded but was very quick in reminding his client that it was Oshún's power and not his that brought about the miracle. He reminded the happy prospective bride that she owed her coming marriage to Oshún and that she should never fail to show her gratitude to the saint, one of the most gracious and also one of the most sensitive of the Yoruba pantheon. It is not very difficult to keep Oshún happy, according to the santeros. It is sufficient to give her a small dish of honey every week and a yellow candle. In exchange for such a small offer the saint will keep a married couple living in harmony and ensure that they will be free from any financial worries. The girl assured the santero that she would not forget his admonitions and gave him a handsome present for all his help. She was married soon after that, and all seemed to indicate that she and her bridegroom would live happily ever after. This, however, was not the case. Although she did not forget her promise to the santero and was careful to honor Oshún in the prescribed manner, her husband did not share her beliefs. One thing led to another, and in the course of a violent argument, he swept Oshún's image off its niche and threw it on the floor, where it was shattered. Aghast at this reckless action, his wife picked up all the various fragments and desperately tried to paste them together, but was unable to do so. Convinced that something dreadful was going to happen, she threw the useless pieces away and hurried to the santero's house at the first opportunity. When he heard the whole story the santero shrugged his shoulders. he told his client that since Oshún had made the marriage, she was entitled to finish it whenever she pleased. The saint had obviously been displeased by the husband's actions and had guided his hand in destroying her own image. In the santero's opinion, the marriage was finished and there was no one who could help, himself included. And indeed, before the year was over, the couple was separated and a divorce followed a few years later.

This example shows the type of relationship that usually exists between a santero and his clients. He takes a real interest in the affairs of his protegés and tries to help them to the best of his abilities. There are of course many people who practice Santería who take advantage of others and charge outrageous prices for useless bits of advice. But in general most santeros are ethical and really devoted to their beliefs.

For the practitioners or sympathizers of Santería it is not always necessary to consult the santero when a problem rears its ugly head. Once the belief in the powers of the saints is firmly established in the subconscious mind, it is possible to ask the help of any of the orishas without the santero's intervention. Sometimes a simple offer such as a color candle can work wonders.

I think it is fitting at this point to state that I have great respect for the beliefs of the religion. I have witnessed too many unexplainable phenomena to have many doubts as to the validity of the magical claims of the santeros. I believe the saints are just so many points of contact with the subconscious mind, each one controlling an aspect of human endeavor. An unshakeable faith and strongly concentrated will could tap the vast reservoir of power which is the subconscious mind, at exactly the point desired, by using a simple key word: the name of the orisha that controls that particular area. I believe this is exactly what the santero does when he invokes an orisha. The spells and the magical rituals he uses are simply additional fuel for his already unwavering faith and determination.

I would like to digress at this point and relate a personal experience that gives some validity to this theory. Several years ago I was living in Vienna, while I was under contract with the United Nations as an associate English editor. At the time, I was having a romance with a young Viennese aristocrat whose mother could not become used to the idea that her son had long outgrown her lap. The situation was hardly an ideal one, and arguments succeeded each other to the point of ennui. It was during the course of one of these arguments that I completely lost my Latin temper and told my paramour that the affair was kaput. I regretted this rash action the moment the words had left my lips, but the damage was already done. The young lord's regal pride was vitally wounded and I knew apologies would be of no avail. Being the victim of a satanic pride myself, I felt this was indeed the death of a beautiful romance. We parted with a cold handshake and some polite remarks on the state of the weather. We did not see each other again after this final argument, but I could not forget him. I thought of countless ways to meet him and show him my repentance in the most abject manner, but I knew I would never carry out my plans and also that he would never return of his own accord. Several months went by and the situation did not change. One evening I went to bed very exhausted, after a particularly trying day, and fell asleep in that very light slumber that is like a semitwilight of the senses, where one seems to be suspended between the conscious and the subconscious worlds. I do not know how long I slept or what awakened me. But suddenly I opened my eyes and to my utter amazement, I heard myself muttering frantically: "Changó, bring Peter back to me on Sunday. Changó, being Peter back to me on Sunday," over and over, through tightly clenched teeth. It was like listening to somebody else speak. It was not "me" who was invoking Changó. It was not the conscious part of my personality, the familiar ego I identify with. It was some primitive and alien entity I had no control over or conscious knowledge of. I sat up in bed, fully awake and badly shaken. Changó is the god of fire, thunder, and lightning, as I have already explained. He is one of the most powerful gods of the Yorubas, and is used in Santería to overcome enemies, as well as for works of passion and desire. Although Oshún is the acknowledged patroness of love and marriage, Changó is the one who brandishes a lightning bolt to overcome recalcitrant lovers. I realized at once I had been working subconsciously to bring back Peter through the power of Changó. My knowledge of Santería and my past experiences with the beliefs and practices of the religion made me feel certain that Peter would come back that Sunday. Feeling more assuaged and relaxed than I had felt in months, I went back to sleep without any further mishaps. This happened on a Tuesday. On the following Sunday I woke up feeling very calm and collected. I dressed carefully and sat down to wait. Around six in the evening, a light rain started to fall, and I could hear soft peals of thunder vibrating in the distance. By nine, the rain had almost stopped, and Vienna was in the clutches of the most magnificent and breathtaking electrical storm I have ever seen. Lightning and thunder followed each other in rapid succession across a starless sky. I opened the French windows of my living room and walked out onto the balcony, impervious to the weather and to the danger of becoming the recipient of a lightning bolt. I stood alone in the dark, my long robe billowing around me in mad swirls, my hair raging with the wind. Every few minutes a shaft of lightning pierced the darkness, framing my silhouette with fingers of fire.

I was in a trance. I felt the mighty power of Changó surging through me and around me. I knew the tempest was the god's answer to my invocation. Peter did not come that night, but I was not disappointed. I knew there had to be a reason for his failure to appear. Next evening I had an early dinner and I lay down for a short nap. At that precise moment the doorbell rang. I knew before I opened the door that it was Peter. He offered no explanation for his absence or for his return. I asked for neither. But I was curious to learn why he had not come on Sunday. He volunteered the information. He told me he had been in Italy over the weekend for business reasons and had just arrived in Vienna a few minutes before.

I showed my gratitude to Changó for his intercession by buying a large red candle in his name and a fresh shiny apple. I had no need to invoke him again after this, at least not consciously.

During this discussion of love magic I have not given many details on the most common love spells of Santería. The reason for this apparent omission is that I have tried to confine the discussion to the mode of operation of the santero and some possible explanations for the success of the magical practices of the religion. A variety of love spells and aids are given in the Appendix.

To Overcome an Enemy

Most of the santeros use Changó in cases where it is necessary to overpower an enemy. Oggun is also used but usually when the purpose is attack rather than defense. Changó's great strength is used most effectively in spells where fire is one of the principal ingredients. The owner of a well-known nightclub in New York told me the following story. Shortly after he purchased his place of business he started to receive a series of anonymous telephone calls threatening his life if he did not sell out or rid himself of his newly acquired nightclub. It did not take him long to discover that the source of the calls was the owner of a rival nightclub in the vicinity. There was only one way my friend could avoid serious trouble, and that was to consult a santero. A few weeks later the other nightclub was devastated by fire. According to the police and to the fire department the fire was caused by faulty wiring. But my friend is firmly convinced that the real cause of the fire was a spell cast by a santero with the help of Changó. This was accomplished by mixing several magical powders together, namely, polvos de *zorra, polvos voladores, azufre, sal pa fuera, powders, precipitado rojo*, and the ashes of a cigar. The mixture was wrapped up in a piece of red silk and then scattered at the suspected enemy's door at the stroke of midnight. A red candle was then lit in Changó's honor and a photograph of the other nightclub was burned in its flame.

The use of magical powders is very popular in Santería. Some of the powders are used to banish enemies and others for love spells. A common practice is to slip the powders in a person's clothing, preferably the shoes. *Precipitado rojo* is used for works of destruction and for protection against enemies. It is one of the most powerful powders used by the santero. Its efficacy and evil qualities are believed to be so strong that the santeros do not like to touch it with their bare hands. It is likened by many to dragons blood, a hard, resinous substance well known in European witchcraft, but I think the differences between both substances are marked. A very popular spell that has this powder as the main ingredient is used to get rid of an enemy in a matter of hours. A lemon is cut in half and a small piece of paper with the name of the person one wishes to be rid of is placed over one of the lemon halves. A tiny pinch of *precipitado rojo* is sprinkled on the paper which is then covered by the other half of the lemon. The two halves are then held together by fifty new pins that are placed all over the lemon in the form of a cross. The lemon is then placed at the bottom of a wide-necked black bottle, filled with an equal mixture of urine, vinegar, and black coffee. The idea behind the spell is that in the same way (sympathetic magic) that the lemon and vinegar are sour and unpleasant to the taste, so will the life of the person bewitched "turn sour and unpleasant." The black coffee is intended to darken the life of the enemy and the urine is used to "dominate and humiliate him." (Incidentally urine is used very often in spells of domination by the santeros) The black bottle with the lemon is then thrown into the river, preferably from a bridge or a high position. The moment the bottle comes in contact with the water the spell comes into effect. Great care must be taken, according to the santeros, as long as the bottle remains in the possession of the one casting the spell. For this incantation is so potent that it can easily backfire unless the bottle is promptly thrown into the river. This spell is one of the few in Santería that does not use an orisha as the source of power.

Another spell, usually employed to kill an enemy, requires the help and acquiescence of Oyá, the patroness of cemeteries. After burning a candle in her name and invoking her repeatedly, the santero may go to the cemetery and bury in a prechosen grave a small box containing the wax image of his enemy dressed with scraps of clothing belonging to the victim. Before this mock burial the santero usually baptizes the doll with the name of his victim. Together with the box he buries several coins with which he pays Oyá for the use of the cemetery grounds.

Death spells are not very popular among the santeros and only a few practitioners of the religion will attempt the destruction of human life. Such practices can lead only to eventual self-destruction, for evil can only engender evil. Most of the real destructive spells used in the Caribbean are practiced by the paleros or *mayomberos*, and will be discussed in detail in Chapter 7.

Money

The first thing to remember if one wants money — and who does not — is not to eat pumpkin in any form. The pumpkin is a symbol of money and belongs exclusively to Oshún. The santeros believe that to give away or to eat pumpkin is an offense of Oshún, who will immediately withdraw her favors from the one who dared partake of the fruit. Once this most important tenet is observed, the santeros can use any of their large array of money spells to ask Oshún for money in more explicit terms. A favorite spell for money involves a small bread roll that is soaked in milk and honey for several days in front of Oshún's image. When the bread has soaked up all the liquid, the santero makes a small hole in the center of the role and places a yellow candle in the opening. He lights the candle in the name of Oshún and invokes the saint to give him the money he needs.

Also very popular in Santería are lodestones, which are kept in pairs (a male and a female stone) for good luck and to attract money. The santero puts the two stones in a glass or earthenware vessel and fills this container with iron scrapings. He adds several coins of different denominations and a bit of fake silver and gold powders. These powders are sold in small bottles and are used very frequently in all types of money spells. Every Friday the lodestones are removed from their container, washed in dry wine, and replaced in the vessel. Many santeros also recommend several needles attached to the lodestones. Whenever the santero wants to attract the love or the good will of somebody, he surreptitiously places one of these needles on the clothing of the person he wants to influence. Dress hems and pant cuffs are favorite hiding places. The needle is believed to be loaded with the strong magnetism of the lodestone, and since the lodestone belongs to the santero, this powerful attraction reverts to him. Lodestones are believed to be such powerful good-luck and money charms that they are one of the most popular items in the santero's list.

Spells for Good Luck

One of the most common practices in Santería to attract good luck is to take special flower and herbal baths known as *despojos*. Usually the santero recommends to his clients a series of baths to dispel evil influences. After this preliminary cleansing, a second series of despojos is advised to attract good vibrations and help solve the problems of the consultant. The most popular plants used to dispel negative vibrations are *pasote, anamú, poleo, paraíso, tártago*, and *rompesaraguey*. The plants are boiled for at least one hour in a large container filled with several gallons of water. The resultant liquid is strained into a clean basin, where it is allowed to cool. After the bath has cooled for several hours, it is usual to add to it several magical substances to strengthen its cleansing powers. Ammonia is considered a superb cleanser of unnatural and vicious spiritual forces, and several drops of this powerfully smelling liquid are invariably added to the despojos. Some other substances used, usually in liquid form, are *balsamo tranquilo, menta, lavándula roja, sal de violeta, esencia de dinero* and *esenciu de la buena suerte*. The bath is then divided into several portions, which are individually used during several consecutive nights. The usual procedure is to stand in a bathtub or shower stall and pour the despojo directly over the head. Very often a special prayer, invoking one of the orishas, is said after the bath by the light of a color candle. The color if the candle must be the same attributed to the orisha who is undertaking the cleansing. Saint Anthony, Saint Michael, and Saint Barbara are invoked very often in this type of despojos. Our Lady of Mercy (Obatalá), the patron(ess) of purity, is also used by many santeros. After the baths are completed and the person is considered cleansed of evil influences, he is advised to undertake the next bath series, which are usually only one or three. These new baths are made of flowers and sweeter herbs, of the kind attributed to the orisha who is being invoked. (As we shall see in the next chapter, each of the saints is believed to "own" a certain number of herbs and plants.) Magical aids are also added to the new baths, the type of substance to be used depending on the needs of the believer. These old-fashioned despojos are becoming so popular that they are being mass produced and sold in eight-ounce bottles. The most popular of these prebottled baths are those of Saint Claire, the Seven African Powers, *rompezaragüey*, and Saint Michael. There are also prebottled despojos for love, money, and general good luck. New in the market are also special soaps bearing the names of some of the saints, especially the Seven African Powers and Changó. There are soaps for love, for gamblers, and for a variety of reasons. The labels on these new products are printed in Spanish and English, which gives an indication of the growth of Santería in the United States.

Another common practice to dispel bad influences are *sahumerios* and *riegos*. The sahumerios are a mixture of incense, storax, mastic, garlic skins, and brown sugar, which is burned over live coals. The resulting fumes are allowed to fill all the corners of the house, especially those in darkened closets and behind doors.

Riegos are undertaken to rid a house of lurking evil spirits. The santero recommends boiling some plants in water, particularly, *paraíso, tártago,* and *romperzaragüey*. The liquid is then sprinkled throughout the house. The best days for both riegos and sahumerios are believed to be Tuesdays and Fridays.

In the house of the santero, and of most practitioners of Santería, there is always present a mysterious bottle full of half-dried plants that crowd each other amidst a greenish liquid. This liquid is usually Florida water to which certain powerful plants and some special substances have been added. After some time, the Florida water is tinted green with the chlorophyll of the plants. The santero uses this liquid to rub his forehead and limbs whenever he is tired or ill, or when he believes he is under psychic attack. The unusual power of this liquid is so marked that it can dispel common headaches, dizziness, and the pain of aching limbs with just a brisk rub. The effects are reputed to be fast and lasting.

The use of specially prepared perfumes for good luck is also very popular in Santería. The santero asks his client to bring to him any favorite scent. To this he adds a number of magical essences, depending on the type of problem being faced by the querent. For love, he may add musk, *lirio, amor, amanza guapo, atractiva,* and *vente conmigo*. He may also use a bit of coral, patchouli, cantharides, brown sugar, a stick of cinnamon, and some rose petals. The resulting fragrance is very heady and musky, and also very effective.

The Jerico rose (*rosa de Jericó*) is very often recommended by the santeros to bring good luck into a person's life. The rose is a botanical curio that is purchased dried, with tightly closed leaves, but which opens fully and regains its green color when it is immersed in water. The rose is believed to be most effective when used in conjunction with the oil that bears its name. A few drops of the oil are placed on the center of the rose, which is then allowed to remain in water for a week. On Fridays, this water is sprinkled throughout the house and fresh water is replaced in the container where the rose is kept. Some santeros believe it is a good practice to write a petition on a small piece of paper, which is then tightly folded and placed on the center of the rose. Such petitions are believed to be granted by the spirit that guards the rose.

Unorthodox Medicine

Many of the people who come to the santero are elderly and infirm, or ailing with some chronic or unusual disease that has been declared incurable by medical doctors. A competent santero is usually able to eradicate all sorts of pathological disorders, ranging from common colds to cancer and epilepsy. The treatment and cure of several types of cancer have been known in Santería for many years. An *iyalocha* (santera) who has cured countless malignant tumors in her lifetime told me of a remarkable cure she made in New York several years ago. It seems that one morning, as she was starting her daily chores around her house, she was visited by a young woman dressed in black, whose haggard face showed signs of intense suffering and distress. When the santera inquired the motive of the woman's visit, she was told that the latter's father was desperately ill with a malignant tumor in the lower intestines and the doctors had declared him a hopeless case. His daughter had heard of the santera's miraculous herbal cures and had come to see her as a last resort. The iyalocha sat down in her small living room and wrote down one word on a piece of paper and gave it to the girl. The word was *higuereta*, which is a tropical plant known in Latin as *ricinus communis*, from which castor oil is processed. The santera instructed the girl to boil the plant in a large container of water and to use the resulting liquid to give her father a series of warm enemas. These enemas were to be administered every three days and no other medicines should be given to the patient. The iyalocha asked the girl to report her father's reaction to this treatment within a month's time. At the end of this time, the girl returned to the santera's house, brimming with enthusiasm. Her father's condition had improved miraculously. He was able to eat for the first time in months, instead of being fed intravenously. The tumor had been dissolved and the pain had disappeared. He was still weak from his long confinement but could already walk around his room without help. He was visibly improving every day. The doctors, who were still checking on the man's condition, were unable to explain his incredible recovery, and were full of speculative theories. The santera told the girl to stop the enemas as she felt sure the girls's father was cured. She refused to accept payment for her help but was happy to receive instead a beautiful statue of Babalú-Ayé (Saint Lazarus), patron of the sick in Santería.

Although *higuereta* has been used as a cure for cancerous growth by santeros from time immemorial, it was only very recently that a scientific investigator discovered the effectiveness of the plant in destroying cancer cells. Doctor Garth Nicholson, of the Salk Institute, La Jolla, California, informed the Science Writers' Seminar of the American Cancer Society that the proteins of the castor-oil plant (*higuereta*) have the ability to agglutinate cancer cells producing their destruction, and thus halting their multiplication patterns. These findings were possible by means of powerful electronic microscopes. These technical details would be meaningless and confusing to the santeros, who, nevertheless, have known of the curative properties of *higuereta* for centuries.

The santera who told me this story has cures for practically every disease known to science, as well as for some that may not be so well known. Her remedies are simple but effective. For recurrent or acute headaches she recommends compresses of black coffee on the forehead, while the patient is lying down. For earaches, she squeezes into the eardrum a few drops of the juice of a large leaf known as *yerba bruja*. She bathes sensitive or irritated eyes with the juice of another leaf known as *malá*. Strong stomach cramps caused by severe indigestion or colitis are relieved at once by drinking a tea made with *yerbabuena*, *ajenjo*, and orange peel. She cures typhus, a plight of the tropics, by giving the patient enemas made of the cactus plant, *malva*, *flaxseed*, and a few drops of olive oil. The high fever that is characteristic of this dreaded disease is lowered by applying to the sole of each foot a strong piece of paper covered with a special grease known as *sebo de flandes*. The greased paper is held in place by a heavy sock. According to this santera the grease "pulls" the fever out of the person's body, while the enema cleanses the body of the disease.

Hot cactus compresses to which olive oil has been added are used to alleviate inflammations of the ovaries. To calm nerves this same santera recommends frequent teas of *yerba mora* (salanum nigrum) or sarsaparilla. The latter is also very popular in the treatment of syphilis. She also cures acute cases of dysentery by boiling a leaf known as *melembre* in a quart of milk. After the milk boils she lets the mixture cool and then dips into it a red-hot iron. She adds some coconut milk and a substance known as *nitro dulce* and places the resulting liquid on her windowsill overnight so that it may "catch the night dew." She feeds a cupful of this brew daily to her patient, who is generally cured by the third day.

In the tropics, where the sun can burn blisters on a sensitive skin in a matter of minutes, the danger of sunstroke is omnipresent. In severe cases, the santeros give a purge prepared by boiling the following herbs in a large pan of water: *caña fístola*, *coitre blanco*, *maná*, *paretaria*, *verdolaga* (purslane), and cactus. The liquid is divided into several doses, which are administered daily until the person is fully recovered.

Another santero can cure even open wounds and broken bones with the help of a few herbs. He told me that a few years ago a young man was brought to his (the santero's) house by two of the young man's friends, who were with him when he became involved in a barroom brawl. In the course of the fight the boy of the story was stabbed repeatedly in the chest and on his left arm, and he was bleeding profusely and was very weak from loss of blood. He did not want to be taken to a hospital because he was afraid he would get in trouble with the police. One of his friends knew of the santero's reputation with herbal cures, and he suggested that they come to the santero's house and ask for help. The santero did not bother to ask any questions. He helped accommodate the wounded man on his couch and set to work right there. He bathed the wounds with warm water and dried them. Then he applied a plaster of crushed chicory leaves and sugar to the wounds and held them in place with strips of clean cloth. He gave his patient a cup of strong black coffee laced with rum and told him to try to sleep. The chicory leaves and the sugar helped coagulate the blood so the bleeding was stopped, and helped promote the healing of the wounds with a minimum risk of infection. The wounded man remained at the santero's house for two weeks, and during this time the santero changed the plaster twice daily. At the end of the two weeks, the wounds were practically healed and the man was able to leave the santero's house.

The same santero mends broken bones with another plaster made by crushing an herb known as *suelda con suelda* and mixing it with a sandy substance called *pedrega*. He applies the plaster directly on the skin over the broken bones and holds it tightly in place with several strips of clean linen. The plaster adheres rapidly to the skin until it is impossible to remove it in any manner whatsoever. It hardens to the consistency of light cement within an hour. The afflicted member must not be moved until the plaster falls off on its own, which usually takes place within several weeks. When the plaster falls off it indicates that the broken bones have mended.

The santeros often use a curative system known as *santigüo*, especially when a young child is the sufferer. Santigüo is a Spanish word that means to bless, to heal by blessing, and that is exactly what the santero does. He blesses the body of the sick person, usually concentrating on the solar plexus or the abdominal area. Generally, the persons who undergo the santigüo are believed to be bewitched or under the influence of the evil eye. Chronic or intestinal disease are also cured with the santigüo. In the latter cases, the santero rubs the stomach with olive oil and *sebo de flandes*, with a curious flexing of the fingers, which are pressed hard and deep into the stomach and then brought downwards to the lower intestines. A candle is lit in the honor of Saint Luis Beltran, and every few minutes the person doing the santigüo stops to bless the stomach and to say a special prayer to the saint. After the santigüo is finished, the abdominal area is covered with a warm piece of flannel. The persons thus treated, usually small children, generally recover from the illness within a few days.

The only son of one of my cousins suffered from violent convulsions since shortly after birth. He was taken to various specialists who diagnosed a rare form of epilepsy. My cousin, who is the child's father and a medical doctor himself, flatly refused to listen to several suggestions to bring the boy to a well-known santero for santigüo. Finally, at the repeated pleas of his wife, who became terrified with the increased violence of the attacks, he relented, and more to assuage her anxiety than because he believed in the santero's powers, he agreed to bring the child to the santero. After examining the child's body thoroughly, the santero pronounced his diagnosis: the boy was the victim of the evil eye. He needed nine santigüos and had to carry the scapularies of Our Lady Of Mt. Carmel (Dadá in the Yoruba myth) for six months. A piece of red linen had to be pinned always to the child's clothing to avert further evil. He was to wear on his left wrist a gold bracelet with a tiny ebony hand and a piece of coral. My cousin scoffed at what he termed a "superstitious rigmarole," but did not object to his wife's determination to carry on the santero's advice. He dutifully brought her and the child to the santero's house every morning during nine days, had the bracelet made to the santero's specifications, and bought the red linen and the scapularies. During the following six months, he and his wife watched their child with anxious eyes, and trembled each time the boy cried or whimpered. But there were no more attacks. Today the boy is sixteen years old, strong and handsome, and the shadow of epilepsy has never again fluttered near him. My cousin, who scoffed at the santero's unorthodox prescription, has become a strong believer in Santería, in spite of his medical degree.

Incubi and Poltergeists — Exorcisms

Among the most common complaints brought to the santero are hauntings and bewitchments. Very often people come to the santero for a *registro*, and find out to their intense discomfort that there is a spirit, usually of the opposite sex, following them around. This is ascertained by the santero by reading the seashells. Sometimes the santero finds that the spirit has been "hired" by an enemy of the consultant to harm him in every possible way. This is known as an *enviación*, which is a Spanish word that means "to send." The spirit, usually the disembodied soul of a madman or a criminal, is invoked and then hired, usually through the evil skills of a *mayombero* or black witch. These lost souls are usually bought with a white candle and a few copper coins. There are also several spiritual entities that are often used in Santería to overcome a person, usually in love spells. The three most popular ones are the Restless Spirit (*Espíritu Intranquilo*), the Dominant Spirit (*Espíritu Dominante*) and the Lonely Spirit (*Anima Sola*). The latter is also known in Santería as *Alabbgwana*, who, according to one of the Yoruba myths, is the mother of Elegguá. There are special prayers, and often artists' conceptions of these spirits, at the *botánicas*.

Although it requires all the santero's skills to rid a person of one of these "tenacious and tenebrous" spirits, they are not as sinister and terrifying as the spirits that haunt a person for "purely personal" reasons. There is a belief in Santería that sometimes during a previous incarnation a person may have hurt or betrayed another, or may have loved and been loved passionately, and may then have become separated by death from the loved one. The feeling of hatred or love can be so strong that, upon dying, the other person goes on to look for his enemy or his lover, as the case may be, in the spirit world. The search may go on for centuries, until one day the object of this intense and undying feeling is finally found. But the disembodied searcher finds to his utter frustration that the soul he has been looking for has been reincarnated, and therefore is, at least temporarily, out of his reach. Determined not to lose sight of his quarry, he prepared to wait patiently for death to reunite them again. Although the unwitting victim of this spiritual surveillance cannot see his pursuer, he starts to notice strange and unexplainable phenomena taking place around him. If the feeling between himself and his spiritual watcher is one of hatred and discord, his life becomes as perfect hell. All his personal and business affairs suddenly become a constant source of frustration and disappointment. If, on the other hand, the connective tie binding him to his ghostly guardian is one of love, he starts noticing that his love life becomes chaotic, as if something or someone wanted him to be alone. In extreme cases, especially in love bonds, the disembodied spirit becomes so impatient and so eager to have an actual confrontation with the living partner that he may materialize and be actually seen by his former lover. Sometimes the spirit actually attempts to have physical contact with the person who is the object of his affection. Belief in these love-hungry spirits dates from the middle ages. They are known as incubi, in the case of a male spirit seeking sexual contact with a living female, and succubi, when a female spirit is in pursuit of a living male. To the santeros, who are not conversant with such terms as incubi and succubi, the latter are simply spirits dating from previous incarnations.

A well-known santero from Chicago, whom I had the opportunity to interview recently, told me of a case he had, not very long ago, of one of these bodiless entities haunting one of his clients. The victim, a young woman in her mid-twenties, came to see the santero in a state of near hysteria. She told him that during the previous month she had been terrified by the feeling of the body of a man lying next to her at night. Whenever she turned on her night light she could not see or feel anyone next to her. But as soon as the light was turned off, she could feel his cold, damp body pressing against hers. When she woke up in the mornings, she always found purple marks wherever she had felt the ghostly contact. After this terrifying experience had been repeated several times, she decided to spend a few weeks with her younger sister who lived nearby. On the first night of her stay at her sister's house, she decided to watch late television, while her sister went to bed early. As she sat down and prepared herself for some badly needed relaxation, she felt someone's presence behind her. Thinking that her sister had changed her mind and had decided to watch television with her, she turned around with a smile, only to find herself facing a tall man, dressed in white, whose strangely vacant eyes stared fixedly at her from a pale, cadaveric face. She jumped up from her seat and ran screaming into her sister's room, but when she returned with her sister to the room where she had seen the apparition, the man had disappeared. Terrified beyond words, she decided to go to sleep immediately by her sister's side, but shortly after they turned out their lights, the doorbell rang. Her sister got out of bed and leaned out the second-story bedroom window to see who was at the door at such a late hour, but she could not see anyone. She returned to bed, but as soon as she was under the covers, the doorbell ran again. This time the girl who was being haunted got up and went to look out the window. And there, by the dim light of the street lamp, stood the same man she had seen a few moments before while she watched television. He glared at her with the same intense, wide-eyed stare that had terrified her earlier. Both sisters spent the night locked in their bedroom, with all the lights turned on, unable to sleep or rest. The next morning, the girl who was the victim of this relentless pursuit decided to pay a visit to the santero, of whom she had heard through a friend, to ask for his help and advice. The santero told her she had to wear a *reguardo*, prepared with Changó as the guardian spirit; she also had to take several purifying baths and make some *sahumerios* in her home. This was only preliminary work, for the actual exorcism of the spirit had to be done by the santero himself, during nine consecutive Fridays at exactly twelve noon. The exorcism was done by dipping a bundle of special herbs, tied with a piece of red string, into a container of holy water and asperging the entire house with it, paying special attention to dark closets and behind closed doors. While he asperged the house, the santero called on Changó to banish the spirit lover, admonishing him to leave his victim in peace. Immediately after the first exorcism, the apparitions and nocturnal visits stopped and the girl was not troubled again by her importunate lover. These exorcisms are known as *despojos* in Santería.

The stories of ghostly lovers are common in Santería. One of my friends, who always laughed and scoffed at all forms of occult practices, was married several years ago, and on her wedding night, while she danced with her bridegroom under a tropical sky, she saw a hideously deformed man come between her and her husband, and kiss her fully on the lips. Revolted and outraged, she cried out and asked her husband to stop the man, but her husband said that he had seen no one. What he did see was his wife's mouth start to swell, slowly at first, then more rapidly, until it became horribly deformed. Just as fast as the swelling started, it began to disappear, until her mouth regained its normal form again. The entire process lasted only a few minutes. But the significant and frightening part of this experience was that it repeated itself every night for a whole week. Although they consulted several specialists, and even a psychologist, no one seemed to have an answer for the awful and repeated occurrences. At the end of the week, they decided to consult an iyalocha, well known for her exorcisms and herbal cures. The santera told my friend that she was being ''visited'' by a former lover from a previous life whom she has wronged badly. The spirit was consumed with hatred and jealousy and would not rest until he had destroyed my friend's marriage. The santera's advice was very simple. She told her client to wear a necklace of red and white beads, to take some purifying baths, and to read Psalm 23 during forty-five consecutive nights. She was also to burn a white candle every night during this period, in the name of her former lover, so that he would forgive her and leave her in peace. These measures being duly taken, the hauntings stopped and there were no more nightly visitations.

Just as there are spirits that are believed to haunt the living, there are others that haunt houses and inanimate objects. These latter are known to many as poltergeists, though in Santería they are called *espíritus traviesos*. The most impressive case of a haunting by a poltergeist that I have ever known happened to a family that lived next to our house when I was a child. The supernatural phenomena started shortly after the only daughter of the family turned fourteen. Suddenly, and unexpectedly, things started to happen. Pots and pans would fly through the house at all times of day or night, pieces of a strange white meat would be found floating in the soup, orange and apple peels would crawl out of the garbage pail, dance their way through the entire house and then return whence they came. The daughter of the family seemed to be the center of this supernatural display, and she was constantly slapped and spanked by invisible hands. A ring she wore on her left hand was moved from finger to finger while she screamed hysterically and her helpless parents watched in horror. Her hair was often put up in curlers while she slept, without waking her up. After several months of this harassment, the family consulted a santero, and asked him to come and exorcise their home. The santero came to the house and asperged the whole place with holy water, did the proper invocations; and to be doubly sure that the haunting spirit would not return, he placed some *guano bendito* (palm leaves given by the Catholic church on Palm Sunday) behind the front door, and a black rag doll dressed in red in the girl's room. (Rag dolls are used very often in Santería to dispel evil influences.) That evening the whole family was awakened by the shattering noise made by all their kitchen utensils being crashed against the walls and the floors. The *guano bendito* was lifted by invisible hands and torn into small pieces. The black rag doll was also ripped apart in front of their eyes and the pieces strewn all over the house. It was obvious that the *espíritu travieso* was extremely displeased with the santero's intervention and had not been affected by the latter's work. The following morning the santero was summoned by the family, and when he learned what had taken place the night before, he shrugged his shoulders and said that the spirit was too strong and could only be banished by a babalawo (the high priest of Santería), or by a priest from the Catholic church. As there were no babalawos living in the vicinity, it seemed more practical to ask a priest to exorcise the house. After some enquiries and considerable pleas and explanations, the head of the family, who was a very influential man with many powerful friends within the Catholic church, finally was given permission to have his house exorcised by an ordained priest. The exorcism was undertaken by a Jesuit priest, who did a full ritualistic banishing ceremony, and exhorted any lurking spirits to leave the premises. The immediate response to the exorcism was a barrage of pots and pans flying in all directions throughout the house. All during the exorcism, the house was beset with rappings, bangings, and howls. The disturbances did not stop until after the priest had left. There was a period of relative silence, as if the poltergeist were taking a breather, and then it all started again with renewed violence. During the next few days, the phenomena became so acute, the family had to leave the house and take up residence at a nearby hotel. Determined not to give in to an ill-mannered ghost, the head of the family decided to find a babalawo who might undertake another exorcism. He found one in Loiza Aldea, a small city in the southern part of Puerto Rico, with a reputation for magic and witchcraft practices. When the babalawo entered the house, the place was cold and silent. There seemed to be a kind of expectancy in the air. The babalawo requested that the whole family, who were still staying at the hotel, be present during the exorcism. As soon as they reentered the house, all the supernatural phenomena started anew. The babalawo took the head of the family aside and told him that while it was true they had an *espíritu travieso* in the house, the spirit got the energy for his heavy pranks from the daughter of the house. The reason why the other two exorcisms had not worked was that they had been directed toward the house alone, and had ignored the source of the problem, which was the girl. The thing to do was exorcise both the house and the girl, which he proceeded to do with consummate expertise. This was the end of all the supernatural phenomena plaguing the family.

The Botánicas

The botánicas are the small religious goods stores scattered throughout the Spanish quarters of the big American cities. Most of the traditional herbs, roots, and plants used in Santería are found in the botánicas, together with special oils, perfumes, essences, incenses, candles, talismans, prayers, and images of saints and a variety of animal products, among which snake skins and smoked possum are very common. The botánicas also sell a powdered type of incense, based on winter bark, patchouli, and sandalwood, which is very strong and fragrant. Also very popular among the santeros is a special tobacco incense which is used in magical works of a particularly strong nature.

Without the botánica, the santero's magic is neutralized, the mayombero's black magic is nonexistent. Understandably, the salesman at a botánica is an apprentice santero himself, with a competent knowledge of all types of herbs and the potential uses of all the magical paraphernalia sold by the store. A salesman at a botánica usually has the names and addresses of several well-known santeros and spiritualists, who can divine the future with the coconut rinds, the seashells, or the Spanish playing cards. Unlike the santero, the spiritualist does not always work with the orishas and very often casts his spells with the aid of Catholic saints that have not been syncretized in the Yoruba tradition.

Although Santería is being extensively practiced in most of the major cities of the United States, New York and Miami remain the most active centers of the cult. Among the hundreds of botánicas found in the New York metropolitan area, the five listed here are the most colorful and well known.

Rendón's West Indies Botanical Garden, 54 East 116th Street This is one of the oldest botánicas in New York City. Its fame is so widespread that the *New York Times* recently published an article about it. The store is owned by two Guatemalan brothers, whose name is almost a household word among santeros and spiritualists.

El Congo Real, 1521 Park Avenue   Although this store is a comparative newcomer among New York's botánicas, it is listed here because of its marked folkloric flavor. This is probably one of the best stores for the typical spells of Santería, as they have some of the most exotic ingredients in the market.

Otto Chicas, 60 East 116th Street   This is the oldest and best known of the New York botánicas. It is bright and colorful and has one of the largest stocks of religious articles in the city.

El Arte Espiritual, 104th Street bet. Park and Lexington Avenues   This store is owned by a sapient and philosophical old man named Don Justo. What Don Justo does not have in his store probably does not exist in Santería. In fact, I have seen articles in this botánica I never heard about before, such as a peculiar looking root known as "the devil's tooth." Don Justo also carries plenty of snake skins which are very popular in Santería to overcome an enemy.

Original Products, 2486 Webster Ave. Bx., N.Y.   This is a busy and seemingly unpretentious store which nevertheless has one of the most varied stocks of magical ingredients in New York. it does both a wholesale and a retail business and caters specifically to the needs and beliefs of Santería.

For a comprehensive list of botánicas in any major city in the United States, the reader is directed to look under Religious Goods in the classified telephone directories.

5
Natural Magic

African magic is natural magic. Its power is the power of the herbs and the trees that are found in the steaming, tropical forests of the Antilles. In these dark, brooding woods, live the spiritual entities of the Yorubas and the Bantus. Everything comes from the forest, from the fertile womb of the earth, say the santeros. Magic cannot be practiced without the help of the woods. The most basic spell in Santería will always require a plant, an herb, a stone, a flower, a fruit or an animal. With *ewe* or *vititi nfinda* (the Yoruba and Congo terms, respectively, for herbs, trees, fruits and plants), the santero cures a simple headache or a malignant tumor. He can also undo an evil spell, drive away bad luck, and neutralize the evil work of an enemy.

The belief in the power of herbs is an intrinsic part of Santería. An old santero I know claims the greatest santero and herbalist of them all was Jesus Christ. With simple and colorful logic, he argues, and I quote him: "To begin with, he was born in a cave, over a bunch of straw. Straw is dried grass and grass is an herb. Then, after he grew up, he spent forty days in the wilderness, without any food and he did not die. Later on, when they captured him, they found him in the woods, praying alone by some olive trees. And the last proof is that he died on top of a mountain, not very far from the woods. So you see, he was always around herbs. He was a santero."

The woods have everything the santero needs to preserve his health and to defend himself against evil. But he must always remember to ask the woods' permission before removing a stone or a leaf from a tree. Above all, he must always pay the forest for whatever he takes, either with rum, tobacco, or a few copper coins.sometimes, when the occasion demands it, a young chicken is sacrificed to the woods, usually at the foot of a large tree, preferably a *ceiba*.

Osain

The owner of the woods is Osain, a one-eyed, one-armed, one-legged god whose symbol is a twisted tree branch. The *ewe* or *vititi nfinda* are the property of Osain, and without enlisting his aid beforehand, it is not possible to do any magic in Santería. Osain was never born. He sprang from the bowels of the earth like Athena from Zeus's forehead. There are countless stories about how Osain lost the missing members of his body. In one of these stories, he was left in these sad conditions during a fight with Changó, who became enraged when Osain pressed his unwelcome advances upon the goddess Oyá. Infuriated with Osain's audacity, Changó blasted him with a shaft of lightning, leaving him lame and half blind for all eternity. But some santeros disclaim this story on the basis that Osain is not interested in sexual activities, as he is a very pure deity and also an old friend of Changó. These santeros explain the missing limbs of Osain with the following story. At one time, Osain was constantly at war with Orúnla, the owner of the Table of Ifá. Orúnla, who is a peaceful god, did not want to fight with Osain but was unable to convey his desire for peace to the recalcitrant orisha. Finally, tired of Osain's constant animosity, Orúnla appealed to Changó to help him with his magic. Changó advised Orúnla to prepare an ebbó with twelve fire torches that had to be lit with twelve flintstones (*odduarás*). While Orúnla was preparing the ebbó, Osain was in the woods looking for herbs with which to harm Orúnla. But the god of divination proved to be the quicker of the two, and he managed to light the torches before Osain came out of the woods. Immediately a bolt of lightning flashed across the sky and fell on the woods, setting it on fire and trapping Osain among the flames. This was how the god of herbs and plants lost his missing limbs.

The twisted tree branch, which is Osain's principal attribute, is used by the god to lean on as he hops about on his one remaining foot. Many santeros keep a twisted branch in their houses in honor of the god and as a safety measure against danger. The branch is believed to whistle when peril is near. It is often lent to young girls who want to ''snare a husband.'' The branch is also used to invoke the god Elegguá, who is said to be a good friend of Osain.

Although Osain is the accepted owner of the woods and the keeper of all secrets of herbal magic, he has to share his natural treasures with all the other orishas. How this came about is the subject of another legend. Changó, who is a great magician and master of witchcraft, complained one day to his concubine Oyá that his ebbós and bilongos were lacking in effectiveness because he needed some herbs to strengthen his spells and Osain would not let him have any. Oyá, who is also a very powerful witch, stood up and began to fan her skirts, until a great gale was created. Osain kept all his herbs in a gigantic gourd that hung from a high tree branch. The wind made the gourd sway violently until it fell to the ground, scattering all the ewe to the four cardinal points. All the orishas hastened to pick up the herbs, which they divided among themselves. From that day onward, although Osain is still considered the official deity of the woods, the other gods can work with herbs the same as he.

The santeros prepare a talisman of Osain which is supposed to have all the power of the orisha. One way to prepare the talisman is inside an earthenware vessel, where the santero places two glass balls, one larger than the other, a deer's horn, some turtle blood, water from the first rains of May, seawater, river water, holy water, and pepper. The vessel is buried under a palm tree to acquire all of Changó's strength, as this orisha ''owns'' the palm tree. Later it is disinterred and buried under a ceiba. It remains six days under each tree. The vessel is then brought to an anthill and later to the crossing of four roads to get the blessing of Eleggúa, who is the master of all roads. From this last burial place, the talisman of Osain comes out fully "baptized," and with all the magic ascribed to the god. Another talisman of Osain is prepared inside a hollow gourd. This "Osain" is said to whistle when danger is near.

The Ceiba

The bombax ceiba, known in botany as the five-leaved, silk-cotton tree, is the sacred tree of Santería and the basis of some of the greatest magic of the cult. No one in Latin America likes to cut down one of these trees, which are considered by many to have great spiritual force. The santeros believe even lightning respects the ceiba because in the tropics the tree is very seldom, if ever, struck by lightning.

According to the legend, during the universal deluge, the ceiba was the only tree that the waters did not dare to cover. All the people and the animals that took refuge under the tree were able to escape, ensuring the survival of life on the planet.

At the foot of the ceiba are buried many of the bilongos and ebbós of Santería. The ground around the tree is always covered with fruit offerings, money, and sacrificed animals. The ceiba is so highly respected by the santeros that they never cross over its shadow without asking its permission beforehand. For the tree is supposed to be very sensitive and is easily offended. When it is angered, it will not give its precious protection to the santero, whose spells will come to naught without it. With the help of the ceiba it is possible to do great beneficial spells for love and, and also for death and destruction. For the tree does not discriminate between good and evil as long as it is paid for its services, and full respect is shown during the transaction. When a santero wants to harm an enemy, he goes to the ceiba at midnight, and taking off his clothes, he walks around the tree several times, brushing the trunk with the tips of his fingers and asking the ceiba to accomplish his will. All magical operations are conducted by means of words and songs. Thus speaking softly and sweetly to the ceiba will compel it to do whatever one asks of it.

The santeros believe the ceiba is a saint. Its spirit is essentially maternal. It is a female tree. Its African name is *Iroko* and it is one of the African aspects of the Conception of Mary. The congos call it *nkunia casa sami* (the tree house of God), *mamá Ungundu,* and *Iggi-Olorun.* The original Iroko is a gigantic species of African mahogany tree that is venerated by many African tribes along the coast of Guinea. Since this tree does not grow in the Caribbean, the African man substituted for it the ceiba, which he rebaptized as Iroko, paying it homage ever since that time.

In Cuba the santeros sacrifice a bull to the ceiba during some of their special ceremonies. They walk in a circle around the tree with the animal before killing it, while carrying lit candles in their hands. Every month white chickens are sacrificed by its roots.

The roots and the leaves of the ceiba are believed to be of great medicinal value, especially in cases of venereal diseases and difficulties in the urinary tract. The leaves are also reputed to be excellent in the treatment of anemia. The bark of the tree is used in a special tea that is believed to make barren women conceive.

The santeros explain that they use the ceiba in six different ways for their magical work: (1) the tree trunk is used to cast evil spells; (2) the bark is used for teas and other medicinal purposes; (3) the shade of the tree attracts the spirits and gives its supernatural strength to all the spells buried underneath it; (4) the roots are used to place the offerings to the ceiba and to receive the blood of sacrificed animals; (5) the earth around the tree is often used in black magic; and (6) the leaves of the tree are used for medicinal purposes, to cast love spells, and to prepare the omiero used during the asiento.

The Palm Tree

The palm tree is almost as powerful as the ceiba in Latin American magic and is believed to be the habitation of Changó. This belief is bases on the fact that the palm tree is often the recipient of lightning bolts, which are the weapon of the god. Lightning is believed by many to be Changó coming home to the palm tree. One of the legends that explains why the palm tree is the constant victim of lightning tells that Changó, who is an incorrigible woman chaser, asked a small lizard to bring a present to one of the god's paramours. The lizard put the gift in its mouth and hurried to the lady's house. Unfortunately, in its haste to get to its destination, it stumbled and swallowed the present, which became stuck in its throat (this explains why the skin of the lizard's neck is distended). When Changó found out that the gift never reached the lady in question, he became enraged with the lizard, and demanded of the terrified messenger why the present had not been delivered. Fire gushed out of Changó's mouth with every word. The lizard was unable to answer because of the pressure of the package on its vocal cords, and trembling with fear it ran up the palm tree to seek refuge among the branches. Changó, believing himself mocked by the lizard, threw a lightning bolt at the tree, which was intended to scorch the lizard. Ever since then, the palm tree has been the target of Changó's anger because the lizard is still hiding there to protect itself against the orisha.

The palm tree is also especially revered by the mayomberos, who use it just as often as the ceiba for their evil spells.

A typical bilongo, used to kill, is known as the *nkangue* of death. With a brand new knife, the mayombero opens the breast of a live black chicken and sprinkles the wound with rum. He puts into the wound pepper and garlic mixed with sulfur and graveyard dust and then wraps the bird in a black cloth. All during this process he is cursing his victim and invoking the spirit of the palm tree (*nsasi*) to kill the unfortunate person in the cruelest and slowest way. He then buries the chicken still alive, under the roots of the palm tree, leaving the head outside the hole. With a new broom (*kamba*), he hits the trunk of the tree so that nsasi, angered at the punishment, will hasten to destroy the intended victim.

A story is told of a mayombero who took revenge on his wife because she had been unfaithful to him with one of his neighbors.

He waited patiently until the woman thought he had forgiven and forgotten the offense, and then came to her house late one night with a wide-necked bottle in his hands. He knocked at her door three times and when she asked from within who was at the door, he captured the sound of her voice inside the bottle, and closing it tightly, hurried away from the house. (This is a common practice among mayomberos, who believe that the voice is the breath of life of a person and by means of which one can kill.) The mayombero of the story went to the palm tree with the bottle, which he promptly buried under the roots of the tree. He then lit four candles and pinned a live black chicken to the tree trunk with a new knife, all the while invoking nsasi to destroy the woman. The very next day the woman responded to the spell by dousing herself with gasoline and setting her body on fire.

Some other rituals use the palm tree to bring rain. During these rituals, the santeros usually invoke Changó or Yemayá, after lighting twelve cotton wicks soaked in olive oil. Another rite for rain consists of making a cross on the ground under the palm tree. Over the cross the santeros build a small mound of earth on top of which they place fruit offerings to Changó and sacrifice a rooster. They light two candles to the orisha, who answers shortly thereafter with heavy rain and peals of thunder and a bolt or two of lightning.

The Cedar Tree

The cedar tree belongs to Changó, and it is used by the santeros to cast their spells when the ceiba or the palm tree are not available. This tree is especially used in the northern United States where the palm tree and the ceiba cannot subsist because of the colder climate.

The Omiero

Earlier, I mentioned the importance of the omiero, the sacred liquid used during the initiation of the santero. Traditionally, the omiero is supposed to be prepared with 101 herbs, all of which are sacred to the most important orishas of the cult. As it is very difficult to find all these herbs, the santeros have reduced the quantity to twenty-one, which are also divided among the orishas. The omiero is prepared with the twenty-one herbs and the following ingredients: rainwater, seawater, and river water, holy water, rum, honey, *manteca de corojo*, cocoa butter, *cascarilla*, pepper, and kola nuts. Some of the blood of the animals sacrificed during the asiento is also added to the liquid.

Before the herbs are added to the waters, they are crushed by hand by a group of iyalochas in an impressive ceremony from which noninitiates (*aleyos*) are rigorously excluded. The ceremony starts with singing in honor of Elegguá and ends with singing in honor of the Ibeyi, the divine twins. The *oriate*, or master of ceremonies, keeps count of the invocations by marking lines on the floor with a piece of chalk after each singing (*ancori*). After the herbs are crushed, they are placed in separate vessels for each orisha and mixed with the various waters. The otanes of the orishas are washed in these liquids, which are then mixed together in a great container with all the other ingredients. The resulting liquid has a very offensive smell, caused by the herbs and the rapidly decomposing blood of the sacrificed animals. Nevertheless, the santeros claim it has great medicinal properties, and everyone present at an asiento eagerly drinks a few mouthfuls of the omiero for good luck and better health.

In the following list I give twenty-one of the most common plants used in the preparation of the omiero, with the names of the orishas who claim them and some of their medicine and/or magical uses.

Plant	English or Latin Equivalent	Owner(s)	Uses
hedionda	cassia occidentalis	Elegguá	against colitis
mora	salanum nigrum	Oggún,	throat infections,
		Yemayá	nerves, skin
			troubles

Plant	English or Latin Equivalent	Owner(s)	Uses
rompe zaraguey	eupatorium odoratum	Changó	against evil
albahaca morada	basil	Oggún, Yemayá	stomach troubles
zarzaparilla	sarsaparilla	Changó	rheumatism, nerves, syphilis
paraiso	melia azederach	Changó	against evil
añil	indigo plant	Yemayá, Oshún	internal tumors, epilepsy
verbena	vervain	Yemayá, Oshún	liver, care of the hair
lechuga	lettuce	Yemayá, Oshún	against evil
yerba buena	mentha sativa	Yemayá,	skin troubles
canela	cinnamon	Oshún	intestinal troubles, love filters
campana	elecampane	Obatalá	bronchitis
higuereta	ricinus communis	Obatalá	diptheria, headaches
algodón	cotton (raw)	Obatalá	bronchitis, asthma, tumors, earaches, etc.
verdolaga	purslane	Yemayá	for good luck
malva té	corcorus siliquosus	Oshún	purifying baths
berro	watercress	Yemayá, Oshún	stomach irritations
anís	aniseed	Oshún	indigestion, hysteria
helecho del rio	river fern	Yemayá Oshún	against evil
calabaza	pumpkin or squash	Oshún	burns, skin diseases, whooping cough
espartillo	sporobolus	Eleggúa Ochosi	against evil

The Legend of the Coconut

According to the Yoruba legend, at one time, *Obi* ("the coconut") was well loved and admired by Olofi, the father and creator of the gods. Obi was just and sincere, with a pure soul and a loving heart. As a reward for Obi's good qualities, Olofi made him shining white all over, and placed him on top of the highest palm tree. But as soon as he found himself in such a high position, Obi became very vain and arrogant. One day he decided to have a party, and asked Elegguá, who was one of his closest friends, to invite all their mutual friends to this feast. Elegguá, who had noticed Obi's radical change, and had noticed how proud and arrogant his friend has become, decided to test Obi's goodwill and invited to the party all the beggars and derelicts that he could find. When Obi saw his beautiful house full of poor, ragged people, dressed in dirty, smelling rags, miserable and unkempt, he almost choked with rage. Sputtering with indignation, he threw them all out of his house and told them never to darken his doorstep again. The unwelcome guests left the party full of shame, and Elegguá, now convinced of Obi's sad change, left with them. A few days later, Olofi asked Elegguá to go to Obi's house to bring him a message. Elegguá refused to go and when Olofi pressed him for a reason, he told the creator what had happened at Obi's party. Deeply saddened with this news, Olofi transformed himself into a beggar and went to knock on Obi's door. When Obi opened the door and saw a ragged mendicant standing there, he told the disguised Olofi to leave immediately and promptly slammed the door in his face. Olofi walked a few steps away from the door, and turning his back on the house, he called Obi in a loud voice saying: ''Obi meye lorí emi ofé,'' that is, ''Obi, look who I really am.'' When Obi saw that the beggar was really Olofi, he was very frightened, and shaking with fear, he pleaded with Olofi to forgive him. But Olofi refused to forgive the offense and condemned Obi to fall from the palm tree and roll on the ground at the mercy of whoever would want to pick him up. He also changed Obi's color, and although his inside remained white, his shell became black and his outer cortex green. The color black symbolized Obi's sin of pride and arrogance and the color green symbolizes the hope that someday Obi will change his ways and become pure again. Olofi also condemned Obi to predict the future. The dry coconut is called *obi güi güi*. From this legend stems the tradition of placing a dry coconut at the feet of

Eleggua's image.

In Santería, the coconut is used in all major ceremonies, and some of the most famous spells of the cult are prepared with this fruit. It is also highly valued as a cure for several diseases, especially renal disorders.

Darle Coco al Santo

This divinatory system means, literally, "give coconut to the saint," and is used by most santeros to ascertain the will of an orisha. To prepare the coconut for divination, it is first necessary to break its hard shell and remove the meat of the fruit. The coconut shell must always be broken with a hard object, such as a hammer. Under no circumstances should it be broken on the floor because this would be an offense to Obi, who is "also a god." After the shell is broken, the pulpy yet firm meat inside is divided into four equal parts, which are then used in divination.

The coconut meat, as everyone knows, is white inside and brown outside. When the coconut pieces are thrown on the floor, they will fall into one of five separate patterns, depending upon which side the pieces fall on. Each pattern has a specific meaning and is interpreted by the santero as the saint's answer to the question being asked. Any of the orishas may be questioned by means of the coconut, but Eleggua is consulted more often than most. Both question and answer must be short and direct. In the following schema we can see the various positions in which the coconut can fall and the name given to each of the patterns.

Interpretations

Alafia It means yes and prognosticates peace and happiness but is only a tentative answer, and to ratify its message the coconut must be read again. This pattern is good if it falls twice or if it is followed by *ellife* or *itagua*, and evil if followed by *oyekun* or *ocana-sode*.

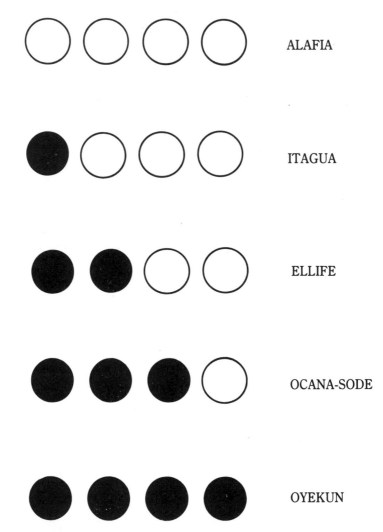

ALAFIA

ITAGUA

ELLIFE

OCANA-SODE

OYEKUN

Itagua It means yes, but it is necessary to ask the same question again. It generally indicates that a mistake has been made somewhere in the divination procedure.

Ellife This is the strongest and most definite answer of the gods. It means yes and prognosticates great happiness. It is not necessary to ask the same question again.

Ocana-Sode It means no and predicts some form of evil for the querent. When this pattern falls it is customary for everyone present at the registro to pull the lobes of their ears and open their eyes wide in order to dispel evil influences.

Oyekun It means no. It is the most evil of the patterns and predicts death and destruction, although not necessarily to the querent. It is usual, when this pattern falls, to light a candle to the dead and to enlist their aid in the problem being faced by the consultant. The coconut pieces are then refreshed by dipping them into a container of fresh water and the question is repeated until the santero is able to get a definite answer. If Oyekun falls twice in a row, it means the consultant is in serious trouble and he or she must sacrifice a chicken to Eleggua and another to Chango, in order to dispel the evil and be protected by the two orishas.

Divination Procedure

Before the coconut pieces are read, the santero sprinkles water three times in front of the god being queried (in this example, we will use Eleggua), and says the following words in Yoruba language:

omi tutu a Eleggua, omi tutu a mi ileis, olodumare modupues . . . boguo yguoro iyalocha babaloche babalawo oluo iku embelese ybae baye tonu . . . boguo yguoro ache semilenu, cosi iku, cosi ano, cosi, allo, cosi ofo, aricubaagua . . .

The four pieces of coconut, which are washed in water before the registro starts, are then examined to ensure they are whole.

This is done because if a piece of coconut that is whole breaks when it touches the floor, it means there is trouble coming to the consultant.

After the coconut is inspected and found in good condition, the santero tears off a bit of the meat from each of the pieces, the number of bits depending on the number assigned to the god he is invoking. For example, if it is Elegguá, he tears off three bits of each piece of coconut, if it is Changó, six bits, for Yemayá, seven bits, for Oshún, five bits, and so on. The santero then sprinkles these bits of coconut over the saint's image and says:

obinu iku, obinu ano, abinu ello, obinu ofo

The four pieces of coconut are held in the left hand, and with the right hand, the floor and the orisha's image are touched three times. The santero then prays to Elegguá.

Elegguá mocueo mocueo unlle obi obi mocueo mocueo

Those present answer, *acuelle*. The santero touches his left hand with his right, and also the floor in front of the saint. He continues to pray.

Acuelle oguo acuelle ono aricubaagua

He puts his hands together in front of his chest and makes the sign of the cross, saying,

unlle obi a Elegguá

Those present answer, *asoñá*. He then throws the coconut on the floor and proceeds to interpret the oracle.

6
The Seven
African Powers

Of all the deities listed in the syncretic mixture, seven have been grouped into a mighty septet known as the Seven African Powers (*Las Siete Potencias Africanas*). The orishas that form this famous group are Obatalá, Changó, Oggún, Orúnla, Yemayá, and Oshún. Although they are also worshipped individually, together they are believed to be immensely powerful. The seven orishas are used by the santeros in very difficult cases. They are believed to control, as a group, every aspect of human life. For example, Obatalá brings peace and harmony among people; Changó gives power over one's enemies and is the symbol of sensual pleasure; Elegguá opens all the doors of opportunity and removes all obstacles; Oshún is the patroness of gold, love, and marriages; Oggún is the god of war and gives work to the unemployed. Thus it is easy to see why the santeros believer the union of the seven orishas beings so much power.

We will now look into the individual legends of each of these seven gods and see how they work in Santería.

Obatalá

According to the legend, when God, the Creator (Olorún-Olofi) became tired of ruling over the earth, he turned his kingdom over to Obatalá. This name is a Yoruba term the means king of purity or whiteness, and white is the color ascribed to the orisha. Obatalá is said to have 24 aspects some them female. In the syncretic mixture the orisha is represented by Our Lady of Mercy.

Some versions of the legend say that Obatalá was created from the mud by olofi. The Yorubas see Obatalá as the protector of cities and temples, and in some paintings he is depicted as a knight with a lance in his hands. The priests of Obatalá are always dressed in white, and often dabs of white paint are worn all over the face and upper part of the body.

The female aspect of Obatalá, also known as Yemmu, is ascribed the same qualities as Aphrodite, the Greek goddess of love. Her love affairs are numerous and some of them are extremely thorny. In one of the legends, she has a very passionate affair with a young hunter, but is caught in the act by Obatalá, who tears her eyes out in a fit of jealousy. For this reason she is sometimes known as Yya Agbe, the blind mother.

The santeros believe that all the bond structure of the body belongs to Obatalá (the bones are white), and also the head and the brains, as well as everything that is white on the earth. The legitimate children of Obatalá are albinos (*talako*), who can see better at night, like the owl, which are also the property of Obatalá.

In another legend, Olofi created the body of man without a head (*ori*), which was added later by Obatalá. The santeros believe that the guardian angel of the head is Eleda. In order to keep Eleda happy it is necessary that he should be refreshed with coconut milk (also belonging to Obatalá) which is poured upon the head every once in a while. When Eleda is allowed to become very hungry or heated, he drinks the blood of the head he is guarding. The person may have a brain hemorrhage or receive a heavy blow on the head so the angel may feast on the blood. The first thing that a babalawo does during a consultation is to learn the state of the Eleda of his consultant. If the Eleda is very heated, he must immediately be refreshed with coconut milk. In very difficult cases, he is fed the blood of pigeons or white hens. This is down by pouring the blood of the birds directly upon the head. This is one of the first ceremonies that takes place before an asiento, when a santero is initiated into the religion.

Obatalá is the god of purity and he is therefore invoked when a person wishes to rid himself of evil influences. In the guemilleres, when an orisha becomes very angry or upset, the santeros invoke Obatalá to pacify the orisha. When there is danger of war or of an epidemic, the santeros place white flags around their houses. Another common practice is to place a few pieces of cocoa butter, coconut and powdered eggshell (*cascarilla*) into a small white bag, which is then passed all the body, invoking Obatalá's help in bringing peace and health.

Cotton is also used in many invocations to Obatalá. The cotton seeds, crushed and mixed with tallow grease (*sebo de flandes*), are used to dissolve tumors. A tea is also prepared with cotton seeds to cure asthma and bronchitis. Sometimes the santeros place cotton over their mouths whenever they speak with Obatalá. He is asked to strengthen the mind when it is exhausted by strenuous mental work. The santeros recommend these prayers with cotton to doctors, writers, lawyers, and all heavy thinkers. They claim the effects are marvelous for the mind.

Elegguá

All the santeros agree without any controversy that, after Obatalá, the most powerful of the orishas is the mischievous and redoubtable Elegguá. Changó's fiery strength, Oggún's talent for war, Yemayá's and Oshún's influence in family or financial matters will come to naught unless Elegguá's goodwill has been previously enlisted. The formidable powers of this orisha are traced back to another legend. Olorún-Olofi, the Eternal Father, was very ill at one time, victim of a mysterious malady that did not let him do his work in the fields. All the orishas had tried to cure him, but without any results, Elegguá was still a child (indeed he is considered to be still a child by many santeros), but he asked to be taken to the Creator, as he claimed he knew how to cure him. He was promptly brought to the divine presence and without any delay he brewed a concoction (ogbo) with a few herbs and gave it to Olofi. Within a few hours, the father of the gods recuperated his health and strength, and full of gratitude to Elegguá, ordered all the other orishas that from that moment onwards Elegguá was to be first god to be honored in any of their ceremonies. He also gave Elegguá a key to all the doors and made him the owner and guardian of every road. Since that time, the power of Elegguá was established. In the güemileres, he is the first one to be honored by the santeros, and before any spell is cast he must be appeased and satisfied, otherwise the results will be nullified. The santeros believe that when Elegguá is happy and propitious, he can modify and improve the most adverse destiny, but when he is offended, he can destroy the most powerful and successful person. if someone fears he is going to be attacked or harmed in any way, all he has to do is make an offering to Elegguá and the orisha will save the person's life.

The origin of Elegguá is very vague. Some santeros claim he is the son of Oyá, who is Oggún's wife and Changó's mistress, but the name of his father is shrouded in mystery. Another version of his origin tells that he is the son of Alabbgwanna, identified by the santeros as the "Lonely Spirit," and who is invoked in desperate cases, especially for love problems. According to this story, as soon as he was old enough to walk, Elegguá tied Alabbgwanna's hands with a chain and wandered off to be on his own. He grew up alone and later on became friends with Oggún, with whom he has had countless adventures. As the friend of Oggún he is known as Eshu Ogguanilebbe, a bloody and cagey being who is the cause of automobile accidents and railroad derailments. Whenever Oggún, who feeds on blood, is hungry, he calls his fearful companion, who slays a dog or causes a fatal accident so that Oggún may eat.

Like some of the other orishas, Elegguá has many aspects, twenty-one in all. The oldest of the Elegguás is Elufe, whose image is carved from a flat, wide stone and kept in the backyards. Anagui, one of the most important aspects of the orisha, is the guardian of the cemetery's doors. He adjudicates and distributes the work of the other Elegguás. Alaroye is a friend of the goddess Oshún and is the one who live behind the doors. Ayeru is the messenger and protector of Ifá. Baraine is

Changó's friend and messenger. But the most respected of
Elegguá's aspects is Eshu. He is a mysterious entity who lurks
in corners and behind doors. As Eshu Oku Oro he controls life
and death. As Eshu Bi, he is the king of mischief and stands in
the corners. As Eshu Alayiki, he is the bringer of the unexpected. But some santeros say that Eshu, without any further
appelatives, is all the twenty-one Elegguás rolled into one.

Elegguá, Oggún, Ochosi (the divine hunter), and Osain are
very close friends. They work together sometimes to create the
most fearful bilongos.

The followers of Elegguá always keep his image in their
houses. The santeros prepare the image of Elegguá according
to the temperament, the guardian angel, and the personal
characteristics of the person for whom it is made. The preparation of Elegguá is a closely guarded secret and only the
santeros and babalawos know how to make it.

Elegguá is usually prepared in the form of a cement head with
eyes, nose and mouth made of cowrie shells. Sometimes it is
prepared in a large seashell, a coconut or a two-faced figure.
The image is kept in a small cabinet near the front door. Every
Monday, and on the third of each month, it is removed from the
cabinet and exposed to the rays of the sun for a few hours before
noon. It is then annointed with a special grease known as
manteca de corojo and replaced in the cabinet. The devotee
pours a bit of water three times on the floor in front of the
image, and filling his mouth with rum, he sprays the stone with
the liquid. he then lights a cigar and blows the smoke toward the
image, as Elegguá is inordinately fond of cigars. The cigar is
placed, still smoking, by the side of the image. Elegguá is then
''fed'' with small pieces of smoked possum, coconut, and a few
grains of corn, which are placed together with some candies
inside the earthenware vessel where the image is kept. A candle
is lit by the cabinet door, which is kept open the whole day.
Whenever food is offered to Elegguá (or to any of the other
orishas), it is convenient to tell the god what type of food he is
consuming. The santero usually adds a few words in Yoruba
language to honor the orisha:

Ala le ele cupaché ago meco
Eleggúa ake boru ake boye, tori
toru la ya fi yoruare

In a more complicated formula, the orisha is asked to protect
the person from death, illness, and trouble and to acquire for
him, his livelihood (*unyéun*), luck (iré), and money (owó).

Eleggúa obara ago kidúa didée emi, fu mi, etié omi, tutu ana, tutu
Eshu, bara kikeño aña agó, cosi aro, cosi iku, cosi eyé, cosi ofó,
cosi arayé, cosi achelú, iré, owó, ilé mi.

Whenever an animal sacrifice is offered to Eleggúa, the
santero who is conducting the sacrifice must remember to say
after killing the animal that it was not him, but Oggún who did
the killing. Oggún, who is the owner of all steel weapons, such
as the sacrificial knife, must take responsibility for all the
sacrifices. The price of an animal sacrifice is $3.15 for each of
the animal's legs.

Eleggúa is syncretized as the Holy Guardian Angel, but many
santeros identify him with Saint Anthony and the Holy Infant of
Atocha.

Changó

The most popular and colorful of the orishas is undoubtedly
Changó, the tempestuous and passionate god of fire and
thunder. The origin of Changó is also the subject of many
controversies, but most of the santeros agree that he is the son
of Yemayá and Aganyú. He is extremely virile and a great ladies'
man. His wife is Oba, but Oshún and Oyá are two of his favorite
concubines. The legends about Changó are so numerous, many
books would be needed to recount them all in style. Therefore
I will confine myself to a few of the most colorful ones.

In the best known of Changó's legends, Oba, syncretized as
Our Lady of Mount Carmel, wanted to ensure Changó's fidelity
in order to keep him for herself. She complained to Oshún about

Changó's constant philandering, without realizing Oshún was one of Changó's outside interests. Oshún told Oba that the best way to keep Changó home was to cut off one of her ears and serve it to the god in soup (*cararu*) made with his favorite okra. Oba listened to this ill-intended advice and very promptly cut off an ear and prepared some soup with it for Changó. When the orisha arrived in the evening, he noticed that Oba's head was covered with a white handkerchief. He questioned her about it as he sat down to eat, but she gave him an evasive answer. He finished his meal and went to pay a visit to Oshún. As soon as the goddess saw him, she told him what Oba has done. Infuriated beyond words, the thunder god returned to his *ilé* and tore off the handkerchief from Oba's head, exposing her mutilated ear. Disgusted with her action, he left the house, and although she still remained his official wife, he never again lived with her. In another version of the same story, it was Oyá and Oshún who told Oba to cut off her ear and serve it to Changó. Oyá, who is Oggún's wife and Changó's favorite concubine, was taken away from Oggún by Changó to avenge an offense of Oggún to Obatalá. The two Orishas have been bitter enemies since that time, and the santeros say that is the reason why iron (Oggún) is a constant target of lightning bolts (Changó).

Oyá is the patroness of fire, and according to the legend it was she who gave the power of fire and lightning to Changó.

In another story, Changó was taken prisoner by some of his enemies and put in jail. He had left at Oyá's house the mortar that he uses to prepare his lightning bolts and was therefore helpless. When Oyá found out that Changó was in jail, she mixed a thunderbolt with his mortar and sent it crashing to her lover's prison, setting the god free. She then flew through the air enveloped in flames and carried Changó away from his enemies in a whirlwind of fire. In still another part of the legend, Oyá saves Changó's life again by dressing him with her clothes disguised, Changó could escape from his enemies, who were posted outside his door waiting for him to leave his *ilé*. The santeros say this is the reason why Changó sometimes dresses as a woman. (Changó is syncretized as Saint Barbara.)

But not always are Changó and Oyá in such harmonious relation. Sometimes they engage in ferocious battles, usually provoked by Changó's roving eye. The result of these battles is always an impasse, as both orishas are equally powerful. Sometimes Changó may win over Oyá by showing her the decapitated head of a sheep, the only thing the goddess fears. Another time, Oyá will win over Changó by showing him a human skull, the one dread of the orisha.

The legend of Changó proceeds from the land of Takua. The god is also known as Alafi and Abakoso. Originally the Table of Ifá belonged to him, but he gave it to Orúnla, in exchange for the gift of the dance. Orúnla, who is a very serious god, had been blessed by Olofi with the ability to dance better than any of the other orishas. All the presents of olofi are like jewels which are worn as adornments when one wishes, but can be disposed of when one wills. Changó, who loves to dance and show off in front of the ladies, did not enjoy having to admit that Orúnla was a better dancer than he. Having noticed that Orúnla seemed to like the Table of Ifá more than he liked to dance, Changó offered Orúnla the magic Table in exchange for the gift to dance. Orúnla, a rather bookish fellow with a deep, introspective mind, and a constant preoccupation with spiritual matters, accepted eagerly, and in due course, acquired such expertise in the interpretation of the oracle, that he soon became one of the most respected and admired of the Yoruba gods. Changó reportedly never regretted the exchange for he became more popular than ever among the ladies, if such a thing were possible for a god as handsome and talented as he is reputed to be.

The objects sacred to Changó are a small castle, which he carries with him wherever he goes, and the mortar with which he makes his lightning bolts. Another of his symbols is a double-edged ax or sword that he uses when he is at war. It is interesting to note that the Catholic image of Saint Barbara has a small castle at her feet, while in her hands she holds a sword and a cup (mortar).

Changó is the only orisha worshipped by the mayomberos, who claim the god was born in the Congo instead of Nigeria.

They call him Nsasi, which is also the African name of the palm tree. His mother is Kalunga, the water goddess of the mayomberos. Nsasi is the king of the mayomberos, the most powerful witch in the whole world, according to the Congos. Changó's color is red, and all the santeros devoted to him always carry something red on their persons. The god is mostly used by the santeros to overcome enemies or to dominate a person. a common protective measure used by an omo-Changó against someone who wants to harm him is to buy some bananas for the god and a big white dish with a red border. He invokes Changó and asks the god to protect his omo-orisha and to punish the enemy. He covers one of the bananas with manteca de corojo and ties it with a red ribbon. He repeats this action with three more bananas, making a total of four, the number of sacred to Changó. Every time he ties a knot in a ribbon, he repeats his invocation to Changó. He places the four bananas thus tied on the dish, lights a candle, and calls on Saint Barbara (Changó) and offers her the bananas, repeating his request. The bananas are left to rot at the feet of her image. When the bananas are entirely rotten, he wraps them in a piece of paper and brings them to a palm tree. He walks away in the complete certainty that Saint Barbara-Changó-Alfi-Abkoso will protect his omo-orisha and will take good care of the enemy with the god's usual swiftness. The santeros say that the genuine omo-Changó is the one who is born already marked by the orisha. The mark is usually a cross on the roof of the mouth. Very often at the hour of birth of an omo-Changó, there is a thunder storm, and lightning flashes across the sky. In some parts of Cuba, the hair of these children is not cut until puberty regardless of sex. Usually the omo-Changós can predict the future with uncanny accuracy. They are able to touch fire with impunity and will not get burned. At a güemilere in New York, I saw an iyalocha, a "daughter" of Changó, possessed by the orisha, wash her arms with alcohol up to her elbows and set them on fire. With her flaming hands she "cleansed" several people present at the ceremony, without burning their clothes or their skin. when she finished, she shook her arms a few times and the flames died out, without leaving any trace of a burn on her arms.

Since Changó is the god of lightning and thunder, nothing could be more natural than to invoke him when there is a severe thunder storm. At this time the santeros recommend burning some of the palm leaves given by the Catholic church on Palm Sunday, as this will pacify Changó, and the tempest will abate. These palm leaves are known as *güano bendito*.

Oggún

Oggún is the god of war and metals. He is the patron of all metal works and gives employment when it is needed. Most of the santeros agree that Oggún is the son of Obatalá and Yemmu, but his true origin is shrouded in mystery. His wife is Oyá, who left him for Changó early in their marriage. Oggún is a very close friend of Elegguá who helps him whenever he is in trouble. In a legend, after Oggún was born, Obatalá abandoned him in the jungle, as the child was the product of an illicit love affair of the orisha. Elegguá was in the vicinity trampling about in the woods, singing, and picking up some herbs. he heard the cry of the child and went to see where the noise came from. He found Oggún at the foot of a tree, adopted him, and raised him in the jungle. The young god grew strong and healthy in the wilderness, and very soon was able to engage in battles with the other gods. His valor was so great that his fame extended very quickly. In one of the legends, Oggún married Yemayá, but soon after their wedding the lust of the battle took hold of him again, and he left her alone for long periods of time to engage in wars against the other orishas. He fought day and night without stopping, except to work at his iron forge. Yemayá pled with him to stop his constant battle, but when he refused she decided to stop him in her own way. As the goddess of the sea, she controls the ocean waters. Therefore, she brought on the universal deluge by letting the sea waves cover the earth. This most definitely put a stop to Oggún's wars, and the god, ashamed at having been overpowered by a woman, returned to the jungle to hide his embarrassment from human eyes. He has remained there ever since.

Oggún, according to the Yoruba myth, taught men how to hunt. His altars are generally placed under some of his favorite trees. Before every hunting expedition, and each time they went to war, the Yorubas invoked the help of Oggún, sacrificing a rooster or a dog in his honor to ensure his help in the struggle. These practices are still observed Africa.

Like most of the orishas, Oggún is also used in difficult cures. A santero of my acquaintance tells this story, which I had already heard on several other occasions. During a güemilere, one of Oggún's omo-orishas became possessed by the god. Thus possessed he approached a woman who had an open ulcer on one of her legs and who had come to the ceremony in hope of being cured. Kneeling on the floor, the omo-Oggún proceeded to clean the sore with his mouth. Another woman, who was standing nearby, could not stand the sight and was sick on the spot. Enraged, the god stopped his cure, and turned the full force of his anger on the unfortunate woman who had dared to interrupt him in such a contemptuous way. He flared at her for having shown repugnance at his action and promised her that very soon she herself would be the subject of the repugnance of others. Shortly afterward, the woman who was cured by Oggún was healed from her ulcer, while the one who vomited at the feet of the orisha became ill with tuberculous. Since this disease is particularly dreaded in the tropics, no one would come near her for fear of contagion. Thus the prophecy of Oggún was fulfilled.

Oggún is one of the most popular and venerated of the orishas, and like Changó, his help is often enlisted to overcome an enemy. The santeros also prepare resguardos using the god to protect their jobs or those of their clients. Oggún is syncretized as Saint Peter of Santería.

Orúnla

According to the Yoruba tradition, Orúnla's greatest power is that of divination. He is also the master of past, present, and future, and so he is the African concept of time. He is the owner of the Table of Ifá, the ABC of Santería, by means of which the babalawos can foretell the future, Orúnla is also known as Orunmila, and is syncretized as Saint Francis of Assissi.

In the legend, Changó was the first owner of the Table of Ifá, but being very young and irresponsible, he did not want to be troubled with it, and therefore he gave it to Orúnla. Another version, which I have already mentioned, says that Changó gave the Table to Orúnla in exchange for Orúnla's great dancing skills.

The best friend of Orúnla and of the babalawo is the irrepressible Eleggúa. In another of the legends, Olorún-Olofi was told that Orúnla was divining with the Table of Ifá. The Creator laughed and said that the only true fortune teller in the world was himself. But since the rumors persisted, he decided to test Orúnla's powers. He convoked all the gods and told them he was going to make believe that he was dead, and that they should call Orúnla and ask him to come and pay his last respects to Olofi. Eleggúa, who was listening as usual behind the door, ran to Orúnla's house before any of the other orishas got there, and told Orúnla of Olofi's plan. When the message came to Orúnla to come and say his final good-bye to the Creator, the orisha approached the imposing catafalque where the false cadaver was lying in state, and said: "Olofi is not *okkuó* (dead). Olofi is *óddara aggadágoddo* (very strong). He only wants to know if Orúnla is really able to see the truth." Olorún-Olofi was naturally very impressed with this "proof" of Orúnla's powers, and gave him many presents and money, which the god very wisely shared with Eleggúa, to ensure the continuance of the latter's help. In some stories, the first fortune teller was Eleggúa, who taught the science of divination to Orúnla and showed him how to foretell the future with the Table of Ifá.

Orúnla is not used for cures or spells like the other orishas. His power is strictly that of divination, and the santeros or babalawos who are devoted to the orisha are usually great adepts at divining the future.

Yemayá

Yemayá is the sea goddess of the Yorubas and has all the mythical attributes of the moon. Her ritual dance simulates the movement of the sea waves. Her favorite color is blue. Syncretized as Our Lady of the Regla, she is one of the most popular and beloved of all the orishas. The santeros see her as a majestic queen, Yemayá Ataramagwa sarabbi Olokun, serious, immensely wealthy with all the riches of the seven seas, and terribly proud and haughty. As Yemayá Achabba, she is very hard and demanding, and listens to her subjects only by turning her back on them. Yemayá Oggutte is virile and violent. In her most proud and arrogant aspect she is called Yemayá Attaramawa. Olokun Yemayá is the deity of the ocean depths. In this aspect she does not take possession of her omo-orishas because, according to the santeros, "the vastness of the seas cannot fit in a human head." Very seldom, a santero will dare to do her ritualistic dance. with his face covered with a veil or a painted mask. But immediately afterward he must say a special prayer so that the goddess will not kill him. Yemayá Olokun can be seen only in dreams. She has a very round face with the tribal marks of the Yoruba (*yeze*) upon her cheeks. Her eyes are very prominent, with long, straight eyelashes. During the new moon the stone (otan) sacred to her is covered with cascarilla ("powdered egg shell"). Before the santero pronounces the name of Yemayá Olokun, he touches the ground with his fingers and kisses the dust thus gathered.

In one of the legends, Changó did not know that Yemayá was his mother, as he had been raised by Obatalá. One night he went to a party, and finding Yemayá among the guests, he was overcome by her unearthly beauty. Unaware that she was his mother, he tried top make love to her. Yemayá, who knew who Changó was, did not tell him she was his mother, but instead feigned interest in his advances and asked him to come home with her. Changó agreed and she took him to the seashore where she had her boat waiting. They both climbed inside and Yemayá rowed until they were at high sea. There she jumped off the boat and stirred the water, creating a gigantic tidal wave that overturned the boat, throwing Changó into the swirling waters. Changó, who does not know how to swim, struggled in the water clamoring to Yemayá to save him. But the goddess let him struggle without attempting to save him. At this critical moment, Obatalá appeared on the scene mounted on a dolphin, and pled with Yemayá to save her drowning son. Yemayá answered: "Alakatta oni feba orissa nigwa." (I will save him when he is ready to drown.) An she waited until Changó was nearly drowned before she pulled him out of the sea into her boat. There she told him this had been his punishment for having dared to make improper advances to his own mother. Changó excused himself humbly: "Coffiéddeno Iyá mi." (I did not know you were my mother.) The mother and son embraced in the boat, and ever since that day, Changó worships Yemayá, who is the only one, besides Obatalá, that Changó considers superior to himself.

Yemayá is often used in fertility rites for women who cannot bear children. She is also the protector of womanhood, and all matters concerning women's affairs are solved with her aid.

Oshún

The goddess of love, marriage, and gold of the Yorubas, and thus of Santería, is Oshún-Yalodde, syncretized as Our Lady of *La Caridad del Cobra*, patroness of Cuba. She is affectionately known as mama Cachita, Yeyé-Cari and Yeyé-maru. She is the goddess of river waters and the Venus of the African continent. She is beautiful and flirtatious and is usually represented with a mirror in her hands, combing her hair with a comb made with seashells. Yeyé-cari abeberiye moroladde codyu alamadde otto: the powers of Oshún are unlimited.

Oshún rules the abdominal area and is often invoked during difficult pregnancies. She is always happy and pleasant and loves to dance and tell jokes at the güemileres, but she is also terrible when her anger is aroused. Lydia Cabrera, in her book on Santería, *El monte*, tells a story about a (santero who incurred

Oshún's anger in a most unfortunate way. it seems the santero was an omo-Oshún, a "son" of the goddess, and had in his possession a yellow silk mantle and a huge peacock, a bird sacred to the orisha, which had been given to the goddess as a present by one of her devotees. Finding himself in dire financial stress, the santero had audacity to sell the peacock and pawn the mantle belonging to Oshún. A few hours after his dastardly deed, the babalawo became possessed by the goddess. Everyone in his vicinity was already in bed when they were awakened by the screams of rage of the goddess, who complained in the bitterest tones about the action of the omo-orisha. Fortunately, there were other santeros living in the area, and they were promptly summoned to come to the santero's aid. Oshún carried on in the most frightening way, cursing her omo-orisha and accusing him of having disposed of her property without her permission. She was in such a furious state she was not aware that she was in possession of the santero and kept asking that he should be brought to her presence so that she could punish him properly. The witnesses of this uncomfortable scene were at a loss as how to explain to the goddess she was "mounted" on the santero she wanted to punish so badly. They decided to tell her he was away on business somewhere, but that as soon as he returned they would tell him of her displeasure. The enraged goddess answered that she would wait for him. Faced by this new complication, the santeros had to pray and plead exceedingly with the orisha to placate her. She was breathing hard, banging her feet on the floor, enraged beyond description, and she finally had to be fanned with the *agbebé* (the fan used with a god becomes very upset). "They are mine, *temí eiyé*, I want my peacock and my mantle," she screamed repeatedly, and only after may invocations did she calm down and agree to leave. But not before she warned them, "Tell him that if he does not return my property, he is going to ikú ("die"). If he has not returned everything in three days he is going to learn who is Yalodde. *Obisú ñañá, niákeni, ofofó, atiyú, afóyuddi.*" (All four-letter words in Yoruba language.) As soon as Oshún was gone, the santeros explained to the unfortunate omo-orisha what had taken place during his possession by the goddess. Two days later he woke up burning with fever, and remembering that Oshún had given him only three days to return her property, he hastened to the pawn shop to redeem the mantle, only to learn it had already been sold. he decided to buy another one of the same color and then went to the market where he bought a small peacock with the last of his money. He returned to the house, shaking with fever, to present the newly acquired objects to Oshún. Believing himself forgiven, he went to bed only to become possessed again by the orisha who was twice as furious as during her first visit. "This is not my peacock," she screamed, "my *aggüeni* was huge. It was *gan-gán*. It was this big," and she exaggeratedly pointed to a distance four feet from the floor. "And this is not my mantle. This is an ugly, cheap mantle that this miserable man bought in the pawn shop." Her fury knew no bounds. She told the santeros who promptly assembled at her screams that the omo-orisha would be thrown in jail for his offense and the he would pay with his life for the insult to her dignity. A few days later the police came looking for the santero who had neglected to pay some bills, and he did spend a few days in jail until his wife could bail him out. Soon afterwards, he developed serious stomach trouble and had to be operated on and nearly died during his hospital confinement. Only the prayers of the other santeros placated the anger of Oshún, and thus the omo-orisha was able to escape what he called a certain death.

According to the legend, Oshún is Changó's sister but also his mistress. She is constantly fighting for his favors with her sister Oyá, who is also one of Changó's concubines. In a story, Changó complained to Oshún that Oyá did not let him leave the house. She knew of his fear of ikú ("death"), and as she is one of the keepers of the cemeteries, she brought numerous skeletons to the house and posted them at every door and window so that Changó could not leave the place. Oshún painted Changó's face with cascarilla and went to the front door to flirt with the ikú that was guarding it. While the skeleton made passes at Oshún, Changó went out of the door disguised with the cascarilla, and was able to escape Oyá.

According to another legend, Oshún made the first lamp with a pumpkin. She always keeps her gold and all her implements for witchcraft inside one of these vegetables. Many of the ebbós prepared under her influence are made with a pumpkin. A popular spell of this type is made to bring back a lover. The santero hollows a pumpkin and puts inside it five nails from a rooster, an egg, pepper, marjoram, Florida water, a personal article of the person and his name written on a piece of paper. He spits three times inside the pumpkin and places it in front of Oshún' image where it remains during ten days. At the end of this period he throws the pumpkin into the river. according to the santeros, this ebbó guarantees the return of the most reluctant lover.

Great evil can also be done with a pumpkin, asserts a santero of my acquaintance, who has told me of a bilongo that uses the leaves of this vegetable. Whenever the santero wants to hurt somebody, he gathers three different types of ashes and wraps them in a pumpkin leaf, together with a personal article of the intended victim, and the latter's name written on a piece of paper. He asks Oshún to turn the life of the person into ashes and buries the leaf in the ground. Soon after this, his enemy dies or is overcome by some terrible fate. The same santero says a bilongo prepared with seven pumpking leaves and twenty-one grains of ground pepper can demolish a building with great ease. Maybe this was the bilongo used against a well-known iyalocha from Delancey Street in New York City, known only as Doña Catalina, who had an argument with another santera, and very shortly afterwards had the unhappy experience to see a car hit the side of her four-story building, which very promptly crumbled to the ground. Fortunately, no one was hurt in the accident and the iyalocha was able, with the help of Oshún, to buy another building in the vicinity.

There are many spells prepared with Oshún's help, some of which are listed in the Appendix.

It is interesting to notice the marked correspondence between the Seven African Powers and some other occult systems. In astrology, the seven Yoruba deities correspond exactly with the attributes of the seven planets of the ancient astrologers. in cabalistic symbolism they occupy the seven lower stations of the tree of life. They also have a startling resemblance to some of gods and goddesses of the Greek pantheon. There are many other correspondences that will seem obvious to the educated reader, but the ones I have mentioned are the most interesting. Table 2 shows these correspondences in detail.

TABLE 2

Cabalistic tree of life	Yoruba god	Greek god	Corresponding planet
Ketyher	—	—	—
Chokmah	—	—	—
Binah	Orúnla	Kronos	Saturn
Chesed	Obatalá	Zeus	Jupiter
Geburah	Oggún	Ares	Mars
Tiphareth	Changó	Helios	Sun
Netzach	Oshún	Aphrodite	Venus
Hod	Elegguá	Hermes	Mercury
Yesod	Yemayá	Artemis	Moon
Malkuth	—	—	—

The dawning of the Aquarian age seems to have brought about a revival of paganism and polytheism. All the systems of occult thought that are becoming popular at present, such as yoga, cabala, and witchcraft, have a polyfaceted array of spiritual entities from whom power is drawn through special rituals. The growing interest in Santería seems to be linked to these new trends in the occult.

Many advocates of the cult believe that Santería is one of the new religions of the Aquarian Age. They believe that the migration of the Yoruba people to the new world was preordained by spiritual forces in order to ensure a widespread belief in the orishas. Some of them go so far as to say that the entire slave trade was conceived as a means to ascertain that the African cults would find roots in the Americas, and from there spread to the rest of the world. This may seem a bit far fetched from a purely rational point of view, but one thing they seem to be right about. The elements contained in Santería will play a major role in the development of the new religious movement which is coming into world consciousness in order to fulfill the deep spiritual needs of mankind.

7
Black Magic —Brujería

Generally the santeros deal only with white magic, that is, the type of natural magic that is used for cures, love spells, protection against enemies, good luck, and so forth. It is not frequently used to attack, cripple, or kill. These activities are connected with black magic or *brujería*, as it is most commonly known in Santería. This type of magic is also known as *palo monte* or *palo mayombe*. The differences between palo monte and palo mayombe are not very marked and will not be discussed in this book. *Palo* is a Spanish word that means branch or tree. Thus palo monte, for instance, is one of the branches or sects of Latin American brujería. In this chapter I will concern myself only with the practices and beliefs of the palo mayombe, from which the word mayombero, or black witch, is derived. The members of this cult are not Yorubas, but Bantus, also known as Congos. Their rites and language are naturally different from those of the Yorubas. The mayombero is very frequently known as *Tata Nkisi* and is feared like a devil incarnate. His power is believed to be real and awesome. A mayombero is not a common delinquent. He can maim and kill with impunity because he cannot be punished by established laws. The mayombero does not invoke the orishas for his evil works, for an orisha is a force of light that can be used only for just purposes. He uses only negative and evil entities for his fearful bilongos or black magic spells.

Following are some of the terms most commonly used among the Congos or mayomberos.

mbua   the evil spirit being used in a bilongo
masango or **uenba**   evil spell
makuto   or protection against evil
ngau   term used by the witch to call his familiar or protective
   evil entity
nkisi spirit
npaka an animal horn filled with a special liquid, used to force
   the nkisi to manifest itself
malembe care, cautiousness
yaya mother, the endearing term used by mayombero to call
   the nkisi
kuna place
ezulu heaven
ntoto earth
ya njila an apology
nsambi kuna ezulu God is in heaven
nsambi kuna ntoto God is in earth
mpambu   the four cardinal points, the crossing of four ways;
   this is the place where the masango is sent to the victim
telemene to spy
telemene nkisi   an order to an evil spirit to spy upon a person
nganga   a big spell to ''tie'' or destroy a person; this term is
   also used to describe the mayombero's cauldron with all its
   magical elements
kisanguele   a species of snake used by the mayombero in
   some of his spells
Tata Nkisi title given to the witch doctor or mayombero
enkangar   to cast a spell

Initiation of a Mayombero

Before his initiation into the palo mayombe, the neophite
must sleep during seven nights under a ceiba. At the end of this
period, he takes some new clothes and brings them to the
cemetery where he buries them in a previously chosen grave.
The clothes remain buried during three Fridays, or twenty-one

days. During this time, the candidate takes a series of purifying baths prepared with several strong herbs, including some leaves from the ceiba. When the twenty-one days are over, he returns to the cemetery, disinters the clothes, and puts them on. He is then taken to a ceiba by his teacher and initiator, and other mayomberos who serve as witnesses. They invoke the spirits of the dead and the spirit of the ceiba to witness and approve the initiation. The initiate's forehead is encircled with a crown of ceiba leaves. The leaves are believed to attract the spirits of the dead, who take possession of the new mayombero, making the initiation a success. A white dish upon which a candle has been lit is placed on the initiate's hands, and he is also given a human tibia wrapped in a black cloth, which is the macabre sceptre (*kisengue*) with which he will rule over the powers of darkness. He is then declared a full-fledged mayombero, and is able to conduct all the fearful ceremonies of the cult.

Before the initiate can really call himself a mayombero, he must prepare, for his use and protection. the legendary cauldron of the Congos, which is known as *nganga*. This frightful concoction is so violently feared in Santería that no one dares speak about it except in whispers. The method of preparation of an nganga has been a closely guarded secret for centuries. I have learned of its connection and uses through a mayombero who asked that his name be kept anonymous, as the making of an nganga is considered unlawful and may be punishable with a fine, imprisonment, or both. The reasons for these stiff penalties will become apparent to the reader when I discuss the making of an nganga.

Moon Influence

Under no circumstances must any serious work in witchcraft be undertaken during the waning period of the moon. In this respect, Congo witchcraft does not differ from European witchcraft, which also hinges strongly on the influence of the moon.

In an African myth, the sun married the moon and they had

many children. The daughters are the stars (*irawo*), and they never went anywhere without their mother. The sons decided to follow their father, and the sun, annoyed by the persistent company of his children, told them sternly to return home at once. The small suns lost their way and fell into the ocean where they drowned. That is the reason why the sun always appears alone in the sky, while the moon is always accompanied by the stars, her daughters.

The waning moon is known as *ochukwa aro*. She is very much feared by the mayomberos, for she is believed to be associated with ikkú ("death"). The waxing moon, on the other hand, is believed to be beneficent, and newborn babies are usually presented to her, after the fortieth day of their birth. It is believed that the moon's rays will protect the child during all its life.

The making of an Nganga

The mayombero waits until the moon is propitious, and then he goes to a cemetery with an assistant. Once there, he sprinkles rum in the form of a cross over a prechosen grave. The grave is opened, and the head, the toes, the fingers, the ribs, and the tibias of the corpse are removed. These graves are chosen ahead of time, and the mayombero usually knows the identity of the cadaver, which is known as *kiyumba*. They are usually recent graves, as the mayombero insists on having a head in which the brain is still present, however decayed. He believes that the brain of the kiyumba can think and thus "act" better. The choice kiyumbas are those belonging to very violent persons, especially those of criminals and of the insane, for the purposes of the mayombero are generally to commit acts of death and destruction. The bodies of white persons are also greatly favored, as the mayombero believes that the brain of the *mundele* ("white person") is easier to influence than that of a black man and that it will follow instructions better. Still, some mayomberos prefer to have the brains of both a white and a black person, to ensure that he will be able to attack anyone, regardless of skin color.

After the macabre remains are removed from their graves, they are wrapped in a black cloth and the mayombero and his helper return to the witch's house. The mayombero lies on the floor. His assistant covers him with a sheet and lights four tapers, which are placed on each side of the mayombero's body, as if he were dead. On the blade of a knife he places seven small heaps of gun powder, which are known as *fula*. The body of the mayombero becomes rigid and then goes into convulsions as the spirit of the kiyumba takes possession of him. The assistant asks the spirit if it is willing to work for the mayombero. If the spirit agrees, all the heaps of gunpowder will ignite spontaneously and simultaneously. If the gunpowder does not burn, the answer is negative and the body remains must be returned to the cemetery.

Once the spirit accepts the pact, the grisly ceremony is ended. The mayombero writes the name of the dead person on a piece of paper and places it at the bottom of a big iron cauldron, together with a few coins, which are the price of the kiyumba's help. The body's remains are added to the cauldron, together with some earth from the grave. The mayombero then makes an incision on his arm with a knife that must have a white handle, and lets a few drops of blood fall into the cauldron, so that the kiyumba may drink and be refreshed. Some mayomberos do not think it is wise to give some of their own blood to the spirit, as it may become addicted to human blood and thus "become a vampire" and eventually destroy the mayombero. These cautious witches think it is safer to sacrifice a rooster to the spirit and thus avoid trouble later on.

After the blood, human or animal, has been sprinkled on the remains, the mayombero adds to the cauldron the wax from a burnt candle, ashes, a cigar butt, and some lime. Also added to the mixture is a piece of bamboo, sealed at both ends with wax, and filled with sand, seawater, and quicksilver. This gives the kiyumba the speed of the quicksilver and the persistence of the sea tides that never rest and are forever in movement. The body of a small black dog is also added to the cauldron to "help the spirit track down its victims.'' Next to the dog, a variety of herbs and tree barks are placed inside the cauldron. The last ingredients to be added are red peppers, chili, garlic, ginger, cinnamon, and rue, together with ants, worms, lizards, termites, bats, frogs, Spanish flies, a tarantula, a centipede, a wasp, and a scorpion. If the nganga is to be used for good purposes, some holy water is added to the cauldron; if both good and evil spells are planned, the nganga is not baptized; it is left neutral so that it may be used for any purpose. After the nganga is ready it is brought back to the cemetery (*nfnda kalunga*) where it is buried and left for three Fridays. Then it is disinterred and taken to the woods where it is again buried for another three Fridays, this time by the side of a ceiba, or any other magical tree. At the end of this combined period of forty-two days, the nganga is taken home by the mayombero, where he again gives it more fresh blood and adds some rum with pepper, dry wine, and Florida water. The nganga is finished and ready to work.

Sometimes the mayombero prepares a nganga without a cauldron. This is called a *boumba*, which is wrapped in a large sheet or placed inside a burlap sack. This sack, with its macabre contents, is known as *macuto*, and it is kept hanging from a beam of the ceiling in the darkest room of the house.

The mayombero believes that his nganga is like a small world that is entirely dominated by him. The kiyumba rules over all the herbs and the animals that live inside the nganga with it. The mayombero in turn rules the kiyumba, who obeys his orders like a faithful dog. The kiyumba is the slave of the mayombero and it is always waiting inside the cauldron or the macuto to carry out his commands.

When the nganga is ready to work, the mayombero tests its powers in several ways. First he takes it to the woods where he buries it under a tree and instructs the kiyumba to dry all the leaves in the tree within a certain period of time. At the end of this time, the mayombero returns to pick up the nganga and to ascertain whether or not it has carried out his instructions. If the leaves are dried, he proceeds to test the nganga further by asking it to destroy a specific animal. If the nganga obeys his command again, the mayombero is satisfied and puts the cauldron or macuto away in a safe place until it is time to use it.

Use of the Nganga

How is the nganga used? Suppose a woman comes to the mayombero and asks him to kill her husband, who is throwing away all his money on other women. The mayombero agrees, for a price. He then goes to the cemetery where he "buys" the life of the man with a silver coin, maybe fifty cents. He pays for the man's life by making a hole in a dark corner of the cemetery and burying the coin inside. This hole becomes the symbolic grave of the man who is to be killed. The mayombero takes some of the earth from this hole and wraps it in a black rag. He takes it home, where he lights a taper that he has previously stolen from a church. He heats a pin, which he uses to run through the body of a live centipede that has been tied with a black thread. He then calls the man's name aloud three times and places the earth from the cemetery into the nganga, together with a piece of clothing of the victim that has been recently worn by him. He takes the nganga and the pin with the centipede to a large tree where he sticks the still squirming animal to the tree bark. He again calls the victim's name aloud and commands the kiyumba to kill the man and to make him suffer the same torments as the centipede pinned to the tree. Invariably, a few days after this frightful spell has been cast, the intended victim dies suddenly and usually in a violent way.

The mayombero does not always use the nganga to kill a person. Sometimes he kills without the nganga. In a typical form of this type of killing, the mayombero goes to the woods where he finds a large tree, preferably the aforementioned ceiba. He sprinkles rum on the tree roots and buries a few coins near it to pay for the work required. He then stabs the tree trunk with a knife and states that the same way he is stabbing the tree trunk, so will the victim be stabbed in the heart and thus killed. The tree is usually stabbed on its four cardinal points. A black candle is then lighted by the tree's roots and allowed to consume itself. The wounds received by the tree will soon be received by the mayombero's victim. Another spell uses a frog (*chula*). A piece of paper with the victim's name is placed inside the frog's mouth with some salt. A handkerchief of the intended victim is then sewn to the frog's mouth. The frog is then put inside a large-necked bottle and left to die in the cemetery. The victim will die at the same time as the frog.

A particularly horrible spell that uses the nganga is employed to destroy the life of an unborn child. The mayombero finds a spider that is about to lay its eggs. He scrapes some bone from the kiyumba's skull and from one of its toes. This bone dust is mixed with the powdered bones of a bat. The mixed bone dusts are sprinkled on the live spider, which is then tied with a black ribbon and stabbed with a steel pin. The mayombero then orders the kiyumba to kill the unborn child the same way he has just killed the spider.

While these spells may seem infamous and horrifying, they are by no means the most terrible spells in the mayombero's list. They are common and ordinary by his standards, and one must remember that in his work of evil, human life has very little value.

The Zarabanda

Very similar to the fearful nganga is another "*prenda*," very popular with the Congos, called *zarabanda*. The basic difference between an nganga and a zarabanda is that while the nganga works directly with the kiyumba, the zarabanda has as its spiritual entity a powerful Congo deity also known as Zarabanda, who is the equivalent of the Yoruba orisha Oggún. Thus Zarabanda is a typical case of a Yoruba god syncretized as a Congo deity (*mpungo*).

The zarabanda is prepared in a manner similar to that of the nganga, but it must always be made inside an iron cauldron, never in a sack like the boumba.

The Ndoki

Perhaps the most evil of all the ngangas is the infernal ndoki, which is prepared by boiling a black cat alive, after torturing the animal for some time. After the cat has boiled for a while, it is removed from the pot and it is buried for twenty-four hours. It is then disinterred, and from its carcass, the mayombero removes a few bones, which he adds to seven phalanges from the little fingers of seven corpses and graveyard dust from seven graves. All these ingredients are placed in the cauldron with garlic and pepper. The mayombero sprinkles rum over the cauldron and blows the smoke of a cigar into its nauseous contents. He then takes the cauldron to the woods where it remains overnight. It is then ready to do its infernal work. This ferocious nganga is an attribute of the devil and it is used exclusively to kill and destroy in the most hair-raising ways.

The Evil Eye

The belief in the evil eye, so widespread throughout the world, is one of the most powerful beliefs in Santería. The santero believes that a person may cast the evil eye without knowing it. Generally such a person feels envy or admiration for someone who is either very beautiful, talented, or lucky. This envy or admiration flows from his eyes in the form of poisoned shafts of evil that sicken and sometimes kill the person thus bewitched. The person who is the victim of the evil eye will quickly lose the quality for which he was envied or admired. Small children are always protected from the dangers of the evil eye by a tiny jet hand and a bit of coral that are usually attached to a gold bracelet. Very common also is the use of a small glass eyeball that is worn pinned to the chest.

The phenomena associated with the evil eye have been the subject of interesting experiments in various institutes and universities in England and in the United States (NASA is also undertaking studies on telepathy and extra sensory perception). It has been found that some persons unconsciously generate more mental energy than others. This extra mental "charge" cannot be controlled by the individual who generates it, and can either positive or negative, the same as an electric current. The mental vibrations thus generated can affect other persons, sometimes with detrimental and even destructive effects.

The Death of the Mayombero

For all his evil deeds, the mayombero often dies a natural death, after a particularly long and busy life. Upon his death, the nganga is either given to one of his disciples or it is brought to the woods where it is dismantled and interred. The best place to bury the nganga thus destroyed is at a busy anthill. The nganga is buried and the ground is sprinkled with rum and the blood of a black chicken. It is left there to return to the earth whence it came. Only after the destruction of the nganga is the frightful work of the mayombero finally ended.

8

Other Aspects of Santería and African Magic

Santería in Brazil

One of the Latin American countries that has felt more strongly the influence of the Yoruba religion has been Brazil. As they did in Cuba and other countries in the Caribbean, the Yorubas syncretized their gods with the Catholic images of Brazil. In the state of Baía, where the cult is strongest, the Yoruba rites are known as *candomlé*. At one time, the practices of the candomblé were illegal in Brazil, and the practitioners of the cult had to flee from the big cities into the darkness and safety of the jungles in order to preserve their religious traditions. The candomblé is an esoteric cult that must not be confused with the ritualistic dances of the negroes of Rio de Janeiro (*afochés*), which are performed as tourist attractions.

The syncretism of the Yoruba deities with the Catholic saints is known in Brazil as *macumba* or *santuario*, which has the same connotation in Portuguese as the Spanish word *Santería*. The difference between Santería and Santuario is very slight. The African names of the gods are almost identical and the legends are the same. To the Brazilian santero, or *pai-de-santo*, the most important saint is Obatalá. Xangó (Changó) is also very popular, and is syncretized as Saint Michael instead of Saint Barbara. Oggún, on the other hand, is identified with Saint George instead of Saint Peter. The powerful Elegguá is known in Brazil as Exu (Echu), the representation of the devil or evil forces. To the Caribbean santero, Echu is only one of the many aspects of Elegguá, but to his Brazilian counterpart, Elegguá and Echu are the same force and extremely evil. In Brazil, Exu is greatly revered, and as in other places in the Caribbean, none of the magical ceremonies are started without first paying homage to the god. Yemanja (Yemayá), is known also as *rainha do mar, mae d'agua* and *Dona Janaina*. On February 2, Brazil celebrates her day with a legal holiday and many colorful festivities. In Baía, thousands of flower garlands are placed on large wooden rafts, which are then floated out to sea. The beaches are crowded on this day by thousands of devotees of the goddess and curious onlookers. The air is fragrant with the scent of fresh flowers, and the sea breezes carry throughout the city the monotonous rhythmic sound of hundreds of *atabaques* (sacred ritual drums), which are played in honor of the orisha. It is interesting to note that February 2 is known in European witchcraft as Candlemas, which is traditionally connected with the celebration of the Moon Goddess's recovery from giving birth to the New Year's Sun God. In the Catholic faith, the same concept is celebrated as the Purification of the Virgin Mary.

The candomblé or santuario, also known as macumba, have ritual ceremonies that are celebrated in special temples known as *terreiros*. Within every terreiro there is a special altar (*pegis*) devoted to the orisha. The initiations into the cult, as well as all the annual ceremonies, are celebrated in the terreiros.

The Brazilian santero, or pai-de-santo, has as his principal responsibility the direction of all the religious ceremonies celebrated in the terreiros. Their *fiestas de santo* are very similar to the gumileres of Caribbean Santería. During this ceremony, the *filhas-de-santo* (female practitioners of the cult), dressed in the various colors attributed to the orishas, stand in the center of the main room of the terreiro, forming a circle around the pai-de-santo. The drummers sit by the sides and the rest of the people stand in the back of the room. The pai-de-santo starts the ceremony with the *despacho*, the ritual offering to Exu. Immediately afterwards, the atabaques start to play and the filhas-de-santo begin their ritual dancing and singing. The dancing becomes progressively more violent and intense without any show of fatigue on the part of the dancers. Soon one or more of the filhas-de-santo become possessed by an orisha and the consultations begin to take place. These ceremonies last all night, until just before daybreak.

The magical practices of the candomblé are known as *ebó*, which is a Yoruba word that means religious sacrifice. The ebós of the candomblé are based, as in Santería, on imitative and sympathetic magic. The spells are sometimes known as *despachos*. A typical despacho is prepared with an earthenware vessel, inside of which have been placed a dead hen or a frog, a piece of bread, a few copper coins and several ants, a centipede and a spider. All these things are well soaked in a special oil known as *aceite de dande*. The vessel is then taken to a crossing of four roads to ask Exu's help in the enterprise. This despacho is generally used to hurt or destroy a person. To accomplish the deed, the despacho must be taken to a place where the intended victim is sure to pass. As soon as the person sees the despacho, which is left in a visible place, the magical force of the spell will take effect. Shortly afterward the person sickens or dies, depending on the strength of the spell. Sometimes a spell is done to transfer the troubles of one person to another. In such cases, the victim must come into physical contact with the despacho, usually by stepping on it.

In Rio de Janeiro, and some southern states of Brazil, the Santuario is influenced by the Bantu tribes or Congos, like the Caribbean palo mayombe. This form of the cult is known as *umbanda*.

Magic in Puerto Rico

The slave trade came to Puerto Rico in the beginning of the sixteenth century, bringing thousands of Yorubas with their religious beliefs and magical rites. Puerto Rico, however, does not have great jungle zones like Cuba and Brazil. The African man could not find refuge in the forests in order to preserve his ancestral rituals. He had to remain in the wide-open areas of the island, and there he was quickly assimilated into the customs and beliefs of the white man, forgetting across the centuries the ancient religion of his African ancestors. By the time slavery was abolished in 1873, the Negro race was completely adapted to the customs of their Spanish and Indian neighbors, and most of the old tribal rites had been forgotten. Nevertheless, the effect of the African cultures left its indelible mark in the music and the folklore of Puerto Rico. The cult of Changó is still a part of Puerto Rican lore. In Lóiza Aldea, the traditional feast of Santiago Apostol (Saint James), patron of Spain, is celebrated from August 25 to August 27, and is reminiscent of the Yoruba feasts dedicated to Changó. During the three days of the feast many of the people of the town dress in colorful costumes and parade through the streets singing and dancing. The dances emulate the triumph of good over evil. There are four types of costumes worn on this day: knights (*caballeros*), devils (*vegigantes*), old men (*viejos*), and *locas* (men dressed as women). The knights dress in colorful vestments of red, green, and yellow, and wear hats adorned with flowers and mirrors. They are a representation of Saint James (Santiago) and carry a wooden sword in their hands with which they fight the vegigantes, who wear devil's masks on their faces, carved from coconut shells. These make-believe battles symbolize the eternal strife between good and evil, which is an intrinsic part of all forms of magic. The vegigantes are known as the little devils of Puerto Rico (*los diablitos de Puerto Rico*), and are very popular in the Caribbean. The day of Santiago is believed to be very propitious for witchcraft, and many bilongos are prepared on this day.

The city of Guayama, in the Southern part of the Island, is known by Puerto Ricans as *la ciudad de los brujos* ("the city of witches"). There are still many descendants from the Yorubas and the Congos in this area, and there are numerous stories about the supernatural powers of the Negroes living in this zone. They are believed to be specialists in the confection of potent brews capable of improving or destroying the life of any person.

I had my first experience with witchcraft when I was a student at the University of Puerto Rico. I was lodging at a student hall in the city of Río Piedras, where the university is located, and very soon I became friendly with one of the local girls. At the time I was having difficulties with my budding romance with a medical student, and as girls are wont to do, I soon confided my love troubles to my new girl friend. She immediately suggested a visit to a witch (*brujo*) of her acquaintance, whom she recommended very highly as he had helped her at one time in a similar situation. My early training in the Catholic faith had left me rather skeptical about such things as witchcraft and spiritualism, but I was young enough to be thrilled at the thought of a visit to a real witch and I agreed to her suggestion. A few days later we went to see the man, who lived in the outskirts of Guayama. He was a gigantic Negro of middle age who lived with his entire family in a small group of wooden huts vaguely reminiscent of an African village. He lived in the largest of these houses, which in Puerto Rico are called *bohíos*, peasant houses with thatched roofs made of palm-tree leaves and floors of hard-packed earth. There were chickens and dogs and a variety of domestic animals roaming freely around the place. I walked into the hut with the brujo while my friend remained outside. He motioned me to sit on a *petate*, a straw mat used for sitting and sleeping, and he proceeded with the consultation. While I explained my problem he busied himself with an improvised altar on the floor, the center of which was a human skull upon which many candles had been burned. When I finished my story, he produced a few pieces of carved bone that looked suspiciously like human phalanxes, and proceeded to throw them on the floor. He repeated this action several times and then said that the spirits had told him that the young man in question liked me very much and that although there was no hope for an eventual union between us, it was very possible to bring him back to me if I did exactly as I was told. With great misgivings I asked what this might be and he put my mind at ease by asking me to bring him three white pigeons, a white candle, seven pennies, and a picture of my boyfriend. Under no circumstances was I to see the young man before I brought these things to the witch.

I agreed to follow his instructions, although with great doubts as to the outcome of the enterprise, and the next day I was back with all the necessary ingredients. The witch took the three pigeons, and tearing their heads off with his hands, he drank the dripping blood from the still quivering bodies. The seven pennies and the picture were buried under the skull, upon which he lit the candle I had brought. He wiped his mouth with his sleeve, and turning to me with a smile, he said all was well and that I should expect my boyfriend before the end of the week, ready to do whatever I asked of him. The cost of the consultation was five dollars. Still shaken with the experience, I walked out of the hut with unsteady legs and hurried back to Río Piedras. By the end of the day I was thoroughly disgusted with myself for having condescended to what I considered pure ignorance and a waste of money. But the evening brought me further food for thought in the form of a frantic phone call from my boyfriend, who apologized profusely for not having called me sooner and who insisted on seeing my right away. As I had been partly to blame for our quarrel and he was extremely proud, I was very surprised at his apologetic attitude. I sat in silence listening to him. Certainly it could have been coincidence. Maybe he would have returned that night even if I had not gone to see the burjo. But still to this day I remember that malicious smile and the blood of the pigeons on the earth-packed floor.

This type of witchcraft is still very popular in Puerto Rico, in spite of the growing sophistication of the island. However, one must be very strongly recommended to a witch or a santero before he or she will agree to cast any spell. The reasons for this cautious attitude on the part of the witches is the constant vigilance of the police, who naturally take a very dim view of such practices. The prices are now considerably higher than five dollars. Some people pay over a thousand dollars for one of these spells, which are sold with a full guarantee that either they work or your money is cheerfully refunded.

On December 28, the island celebrates the Day of the Innocents, when, according to the legend, Herod had thousands of children massacred in Jerusalem. On this day, there is dancing in the streets of the small towns, and men dressed in colorful costumes with masks on their faces roam about in groups dancing and singing from house to house. This is the equivalent of April Fool's Day and all sorts of tricks and jokes are played on Friends and relatives. This day is considered very ''witchy,'' and any spell, or *amarre*, cast under its influence is believed to be very efficacious. Another day when supernatural forces are believed to be very strong is June 24, the day of Saint John the Baptist, the patron saint of Puerto Rico. On this day many spells are traditionally cast, and many forms of divination are undertaken, especially by young, unmarried women. Among the divinations of this day there is one by means of which a girl can learn whether her future husband will be rich or poor. She takes three potatoes, peels one completely, peels only half of another, and the last one is left unpeeled. The potatoes are placed under her bed on the eve of the twenty-fourth. The next morning, she reaches under her bed and picks one of the potatoes at random. The potato that is completely peeled means her husband will be poor, the half-peeled potato, that he will be of middle class, and the unpeeled potato, that he will be rich. Another divination uses the white of an egg, which is placed inside a glass full of water. Upon awakening, the girl tries to decipher from the shape assumed by the egg white what her immediate destiny is going to be. A church means a weeding; a ship, that she will travel; a coffin, a death in the family; and so on. Still another divination requires the use of several needles and a pan of water. The larger needle represents the girl who is asking the question. The smaller needles are identified with the girl's suitors. She puts the needles in the water and watches them to see which of the smaller needles touches the large one. This means that particular man loves her very much. My mother taught me a short prayer to Saint George, which is also said on the eve of June 24. In the prayer the girl asks Saint George to show her in a dream the man she is going to marry. It is important that she eat a very salty egg before going to sleep, and she must be in bed before midnight.

Another traditional custom of this day is to take a bath in

seawater, which is considered a rebaptism under the powerful influence of Saint John the Baptist. For this reason, the beaches of Puerto Rico are always overly crowded on June 24.

One of the Catholic saints most commonly used in all sorts of spells is Saint Anthony, known as the "bread giver" and the finder of lost things." there is always a small loaf of bread in front of Saint Anthony's image to ensure that there will always be money and food in the house. The saint is also used very often in love problems. A very common practice among girls who want to trap a husband is to turn the image of the saint upside down until he brings them a husband or a steady lover. Saint Martha and Saint Elena are also very popular in love matters. Saint Claire is used to cleanse away evil and to solve problems. A sell-known ebbó using her help is prepared by filling a glass with water and putting an egg inside the glass. A special prayer is said to the saint with a white candle during nine days. At the end of this period of time the water is thrown into the street and the egg is brought to a park where it is crashed on the ground. It is believed that as the egg breaks, all the trouble surrounding the person will be dispersed. Saint Michael is believed to be extremely powerful in overcoming enemies. There is a very famous prayer used for this purpose known as the "revocation" of Saint Michael. The person casting the spell fills a glass with water and salt and puts the name of his enemy, written on a piece of paper, inside the glass. He then covers the glass tightly with a saucer and turns the glass over until it sits upside down over the saucer, ensuring the water stays inside the glass. A white candle is divided into nine pieces, and every night during nine days, a piece is burned in honor of Saint Michael on top of the glass, while saying the prayer. The aim of the spell is to send back to the enemy any evil thoughts or intentions he has against the person casting the spell.

Most saints have special prayers that are traditionally associated with them. The prayers are printed on loose leaves and can be purchased at any botánica.

The "irreverent" uses of the Catholic saints and the deeply rooted beliefs in spiritualism and witchcraft throughout the island have been a thorn in the side of the Catholic church for many centuries. I remember, as a child, the sermons of our parish priest against the evils of Satan, who tempted good Catholics into the black practices of spiritualism and witchcraft. He used to preach against superstition and idolatry until he grew red in the face. Everyone would listen respectfully to his sermons and agree with him on the truth of his words. But he knew that in spirit of all this apparent agreement, over one-half of his parish practiced spiritualism and witchcraft behind his back. Today the Catholic church has become more lenient with these practices, even without condoning them, maybe because it recognizes the futility of trying to efface them. In any case, I was not too surprised a few years ago when a well-known spiritualist told me one of her parish priests had asked her to help him with one of her spells so that he would survive a major operation he had to undergo.

Holy Week

Two of the most important days for the practitioners of Santería are Good Friday and Saturday of Glory. The santeros believe that on Good Friday God is absent from the earth. He cannot or will not stop evil from taking form. For that reason, the mayomberos feel free to do some of their most maleficent works on this day. They collect herbs for evil purposes, feed blood to their ngangas, and conduct all sorts of diabolical transactions with the powers of darkness. A typical way to conduct such a transaction is to go with a mirror to a river. The mirror is held in such a way that it reflects the water upon its surface. Immediately afterwards, the face of the mirror will darken and Satan win manifest himself through the glass.

Early the next day, on Saturday of Glory, nature comes back to life, and the santeros are able to practice their white magic again. They go to the woods before the sun comes up and cut all the herbs and plants they will need for their magical practices during the year. These herbs are believed to be very magical as they are full with the aché ("strength, grace") of the resurrected Christ. Many santeros keep the ewe they collect on this day in a cool place inside their houses. When the first rains of May come, they gather some of the rainwater and boil the herbs in it. The liquid is kept in a big container and it is reputed to cure many diseases.

The Commercial Side of Santería

The true santero, the one who has been initiated in the mysteries of the religion and has "made the saint," is very powerful and influential in the Spanish communities. Hundreds of people come to him for a registro each month. While the price for the consultation is not very high, the remedies prescribed by the santero may cost hundreds of dollars. The people who come to the santero for advice are usually in difficult or even critical situations, and having found no solution to their problems in a natural way, they resort to occult means to relieve their anxieties. These persons are often the victims of unscrupulous santeros who charge them outrageous prices to solve their problems. The honest and dedicated practitioners of the religion, and there are quite a few of them, will not accept any rewards for their work. The registro must be paid because the money charged, usually $1.15, is needed to buy candles for the orisha who was consulted during the registro. Other than that, the true santero will not take any money from the consultant, except the amounts necessary to buy the ingredients of the spells and the animals required in the sacrifices.

What makes Santería such a profitable business is the undeniable and peculiar powers of the santero. Whether or not he is honest, most of the time his spells do seem to work. The more accurate his predictions and spells prove to be, the quicker his fame will spread. In Puerto Rico, the santeros do very steady business with people in the theatrical and business worlds. Aspiring young actors and actresses flock to the houses of the santeros in the hope of assuring a successful career for themselves. Gamblers, businessmen in dire financial stress, young women in search of a husband, wives with philandering husbands all come to the santero for help and advice. Highly successful santeros become rich very rapidly. They own real estate, profitable businesses, and have staggering bank accounts. A well-known and very expensive ebbó to ensure luck and money uses the goddess Oshún and costs $1,540. By means of this spell, the santero transfers Oshún's power over money to his client. The people who buy this spell are mostly businessmen who want to expand their wealth. It is considered an investment, the same as buying shares in the stock market. And more often than not, it proves to be a successful investment, for this ebbó is reputed to have made the fortunes of a great many people.

It is not uncommon for the santero to get requests to kill people. Although the darker side of African magic is reserved for the mayomberos, or black witches, there are santeros who, for the right price, will undertake the destruction of human life. A santero told me that not very long ago the wife of a well-known Latin American singer came to see him with the request that he kill the illegitimate, newborn son of her husband. It seems she was unable to bear children and was afraid the new child would bring about the destruction of her marriage. She offered five thousand dollars to the santero to commit this crime. He told her that his powers were not intended for such proposes and that she would do much better if she went to see a mayombero, who specializes in that type of work. Shortly afterward he learned through another santero that this woman succeeded in finding a black witch and that the child had died of a sudden respiratory illness.

It is difficult for the logical Western mind to accept that such things as magic spells and witchcraft can alter human life. Anything that cannot be explained by deductive logic and analytical reasoning is unacceptable to the educated mind. Yet, ritual magic and primitive beliefs have been the subject of interesting speculations by some of the world's foremost psychoanalysts. Carl G. Jung was a great student of the occult and he theorized, and endeavored to prove scientifically, that all the phenomena associated with occult practices are deeply rooted in the unconscious mind. The awesome powers of the human mind have long been accepted by psychologists. The speculations now are not whether these powers exist, but rather how are they developed and how far do they extend. From a psychological point of view, the strange powers of the santero lie deeply imbedded in what Jung called the "collective unconscious," that is, that part of the human psyche that retains and transmits the "common psychological inheritance of mankind." The santero is an intensely aware human being, who has become thoroughly identified with nature, artfully penetrating her deepest secrets. And since the unconscious is a natural phenomenon, the santero can rightfully claim his share of the cosmic inheritance, and in his microcosmic way, affect and control the natural laws. Any of us can accomplish the same, whenever we are ready to merge with the soul of nature.

Appendix

Magic Spells of Santería

The ingredients used by the santeros in their spells are carefully chosen, and always bear a distinct relation to the nature of the problem. All the materials employed in the *ebbós* and *bilongos* give a clue to their uses either through their names or their individual characteristics and composition. Each spell mimics an actual human experience, usually the one the santero wants his client to undergo. On the principle that like produces like, many things are done by him in deliberate imitation of the result he wishes to attain. Each spell is a miniature drama staged by the santero, using the ingredients of the spell to represent the persons involved or what he wants them to experience. The stories told by the spells may be of love, of hatred, or of hope. The forces used to turn these staged productions into reality are the supernatural powers of the Yoruba gods. Once the santero's attention is riveted on a given situation that he wishes to change for his or his client's benefit, the spark that promotes the desired effect is the total conviction and intense faith of the santero in the power of the orishas and the righteousness of his demands. This duality of belief is so powerful that it releases vast amounts of energy, which in turn bring about the sought-for reaction.

The spell of the "drunken coconut," listed in the Appendix under Love Spells, is a good example of this peculiarity of the sympathetic magic of Santería. This spell calls for the use of a coconut, various types of liquor, candies, the smoke of a heavy cigar, and several essences. The names of the essences are:

amor   love
dominante   dominant
menta   mint
sígueme   follow me
vencedora   triumphant

Menta is traditionally associated with spells designed to overcome somebody's mind. The obvious reason for this practice is the similarity between the Spanish words *menta* ("mint") and *mente* ("mind"). *Amoníaco* or *armoníaco* (ammonia) is used by many santeros, mixed with sugar, to promote harmonious relations between two persons. Why? Because *armoníaco* is very similar to armonía ("harmony") — and, of course, sugar is natural sweetener.

In the spell of the "drunken coconut," the coconut symbolizes the head and the mind of the person who is the subject of the spell. The coconut shell is emptied of its milk; this action represents a form of mental catharsis whereby all the person's previous beliefs and ideas are disposed of. The empty shell is then filled with candies to sweeten the victim's disposition toward the one who is casting the spell. Several types of liquor are added to make the victim "drunk" with the love suggested by the love essence, and so completely dazed and weak-willed, he will be unable to resist the subtle suggestions of the other essences that seem to whisper: "*Follow me*, for I am *triumphant* and *dominant* over your *mind* with my *love*.*" The smoke of the cigar further contributes to the victim's spiritual and mental giddiness, and renders him an easy prey to the santero's will. The orisha invoked in this spell is the mighty Eleggua, who as the master of all doors can certainly lock and unlock a person's mind whenever he so chooses. The candles serve to reinforce the spell and the will of the santero.

This spell is obviously an application of the law of similarity, which is the basis of homeopathic magic. It is a typical example of the symbolic imagery used by the santero in his magical work. Carl G. Jung, in his book *Man and His Symbols*, said that "symbols always stand for something more than their obvious and immediate meaning. Furthermore, they are natural and spontaneous products. They appear in all kinds of psychic manifestations. There are symbolic thoughts and feelings, symbolic acts and situations. It often seems that even inanimate objects co-operate with the unconscious in the arrangement of symbolic patterns. There are many symbols, however, that are not individual but collective in their nature and origin. These are chiefly religious images, emanating from primeval dreams and creative fantasies. As such, these images are involuntary, spontaneous manifestations and by no means intentional inventions.

This fact is of great importance in understanding the underlying motivations of the santero and his spell casting. For the origins of the religious beliefs and practices of Santería are "so far buried in the mystery of the past that they seem to have no human source." They are in fact "collective representations" and as such they come through to the conscious levels when the mind is in a receptive state. This is what happens when the santero invokes an orisha to conduct a ritual or to cast a spell. He touches the hidden lock of the unconscious, thereby releasing a stream of symbolic imaginary that he interprets as the format for his spell or for his ritual.

The spells listed in the Appendix have been divided into several categories, namely, those for love, for money, for good luck, and to dispel evil influences. They represent a cross section of the more traditional and reputedly effective spells of Santería.

(All the ingredients used in these spells can be found at any well-stocked botánica.)

FOR LOVE

One very mild suggestion is to cook a hamburger patty that has been impregnated with the body's fluids (sweat) and serve it to the person desired.

FOR LOVE

To set the mood for love, modern santeros recommend the use of a prebottled love bath (*despojo de amor*) and a love soap. The despojo is added to a half tub of warm water where the person soaks for at least half an hour. The air is then sprayed with a love incense spray, and a red candle is lit in honor of Changó, the patron of passion and desire. The santeros also advise keeping a small stick of cinnamon in the mouth during any love encounter, as the cinnamon is believed to have great seduction powers.

FOR LOVE

A triangle is formed with three corn husks. The first and last names of the person to be bewitched are written on two separate pieces of paper, which are placed in the form of a cross in the center of the triangle. A candle is lit on top of the two papers and the word *Nfuriri* is repeated three times.

FOR LOVE

A common practice to win somebody's favors is to tie five of his or her hairs with five hairs from the person who is casting the spell. The hairs are placed in the form of a cross in the center of a small bread roll, which is then buried in a flower pot filled with four different types of earth. A sprig of rue is planted in the pot in the name of Oshún, asking her that in the same way the rue grows inside the pot, so will love grow in the heart of the victim for the person who desires him or her.

FOR LOVE

A green candle is burnt in Saint Martha's honor during nine days, asking her intercession in winning the love of the person desired. Saint Martha, who, according to the legend, could "conquer dragons and wild beasts," is also asked that she will so dominate the bewitched person that he (or she) will not be able to eat or sleep until he (or she) comes to the person who is casting the spell. A special prayer to Saint Martha is sold in the botánicas, as well as a gold-plated, tiny dragon bearing her name.

FOR LOVE

A small bowl is half filled with water to which are added some sprigs of *yerbabuena,* a tablespoon of honey, some sugar, seven cloves, and Florida water. A white candle, around which a piece of white ribbon has been tied, is placed in the center of the bowl and lit in the name of Saint Elena. This saint is also very popular in love spells and is believed to grant any love request. She should be invoked and asked that in the same way the ribbon is tied around the candle, so will she tie together the destinies of the petitioner and the person he or she wants. The candle is then removed from the liquid and allowed to burn outside the bowl. The liquid is used in a bath. The spell is repeated during seven consecutive days.

FOR LOVE

This spell is known as "the drunken coconut." It is an offer to Elegguá to enlist his aid in winning the love of a person. One starts by sawing off the top of a coconut and throwing away its milk. The empty coconut shell is filled with caramels, gumdrops,and five types of liquor. Several essences are also added to the mixture, namely, *esencia de menta, de amor, dominante, vencedora,* and *sígueme.* A cigar is lit in Elegguá's name and the smoke is blown inside the coconut shell. The top of the shell is replaced before the smoke can be dispersed, and the two parts of the coconut are sealed together with the wax from a candle bought in a church. The coconut symbolizes the head of the person who is being bewitched. A white candle is lit in Elegguá's honor during five consecutive days, asking the orisha for the love of the person desired.

FOR LOVE

This spell requires the help of Changó. The top of an apple is removed and a piece of paper with the name of the person desired is placed inside the hollowed fruit. The hole is then filled with honey and the top of the apple is replaced. The fruit is placed in front of an image of Changó (Saint Barbara), and a red candle is lit in honor of the orisha during nine days, asking him to sweeten the disposition of the person bewitched and to fill his heart with love for the petitioner.

LOVE PERFUME

The santeros recommend simply adding the following ingredients to any favorite perfume:

valeriana sugar
mastuerzo cinnamon
polvo de imán a bit of coral
zun-zún a gardenia

LOVE PERFUME

This perfume is prepared with seven essences or perfumes, seven herbs of flowers, and seven other ingredients.

Herbs or flowers	Essences or perfumes
mastuerzo	*Loción de Pompeya*
paraíso	*Una Gota de Amor*
yerba dulce	*esencia atractiva*
yerba bruja	*esencia de amor*
yerba linda	*esencia imán*
rose petals	*esencia amarra hombre*
azucenas (white lily)	*esencia de mosca* (musk)

Other Ingredients

Cantharides	brown sugar
coral	cloves
a bit of quicksilver	a few drops of
cinnamon	menstrual blood

All the ingredients are placed together inside a wide-necked bottle, which must not be touched during seven days. At the end of this period, the perfume is strained and transferred to another bottle. It is ready to be used. The resulting scent is soft and musky, but very rich and provocative.

LOVE BATH

The more traditional santeros scoff at the use of prebottled baths. They insist the good-luck baths should be prepared with fresh plants and flowers. A typical love bath is prepared with the following ingredients:

5 yellow roses	*esencia de amor*
paraíso	*esencia atractiva*
cloves	*esencia dominante*
cinnamon	*esencia vente conmigo*
honey	*esencia vencedora*

The roses and the paraíso (a plant) are boiled for an hour in a large container of water, together with the cloves and all the other ingredients are added. The bath is then poured over the head and the entire procedure is repeated during five days. It is very helpful to invoke the goddess Oshún and to light a yellow candle in her honor after the bath.

TO BRING BACK A LOVER

A small pumpkin is hollowed and inside are placed five nails from a rooster, an egg, some pepper, marjoram, Florida water, and the name of the person to be bewitched written on a small piece of paper. It is also important to include among the ingredients a used personal article of the victim. The person who is casting the spell must spit inside the pumpkin and offer it to Oshún. It is left in front of the orisha's image during nine days. After this time it is thrown into the river. The person desired usually returns within five days after this spell is finished.

TO BRING BACK A LOVER

The names of the two lovers are written on a piece of parchment with blood that has been drawn from the middle finger with the help of a needle (never a pin). The names must be written in a small circle and surrounded with three circles of blood. The parchment is then folded and buried in the ground at exactly nine in the evening. The best day for the spell is Friday.

TO RENEW A LOVE AFFAIR

The santeros claim that the best way to resume a love affair is to pay a visit to the estranged lover and to distribute ten grains of pepper along the way, asking Elegguá's help in making the person happy and eager to renew the relationship.

TO ENSURE A LOVER'S FIDELITY

Some of the victim's hairs are burned and sprinkled over a chair or sofa that has been previously rubbed with honey. It is important that the person to be bewitched sits in the chair as soon as possible.

TO GET MARRIED

A used personal article of the person desired is tied around the belly of a frog and secured with a red and a black ribbon. The frog is placed inside a cardboard box that has been pierced in several places so that the frog may breathe. The guardian angel of the victim is invoked and asked to intercede and bring about a prompt marriage between the latter and the petitioner. Otherwise the bewitched person will suffer the same torments as the frog, which will be allowed to die of hunger and thirst. Invariably the victim of the spell becomes obsessed with the thought of marrying the person who is bewitching him, and the marriage takes place soon thereafter.

TO GET MARRIED

The name of the person desired is written on a piece of paper, which is then placed at the bottom of a small glass bowl. Over the paper are arranged five small books. The bowl is filled with honey and offered to Oshún, patroness of marriage, being careful to taste the honey at the moment of the offer. A yellow candle is lit in the orisha's honor during five days, asking her to propitiate the marriage. It is helpful to purchase a small image of the saint prior to the ceremony.

TO GET MARRIED

This spell was designed to force a reluctant man into marriage. The main ingredient of the spell is the man's sperm, which must be gathered surreptitiously in a small wad of cotton without him knowing what it is intended for. The cotton is formed into a wick by rolling it between the fingers until some of it protrudes from the rest of the cotton. This crude wick is used in oil lamp that requires the following ingredients:

a large lily bulb	*aceite de amor*
aceite de coco	*aceite amarra hombre*
aceite de menta	*aceite de lirio*
aceite intranquilo	cantharides
aceite yo puedo y tu no	quicksilver

The top of the lily is removed with a knife and the bulb is hollowed by removing most of its meat, ensuring that the outer cortex is intact. At the bottom of the cavity is placed a piece of parchment with the man's name written across it in the form of a cross. The quicksilver is added with the intention that in the same way this liquid runs, so will the man run to the woman who wants him. The cantharides are believed to fill the man with the desire for the woman who is bewitching him. A little of each of the oils is added until the bulb is almost filled. The cotton wad is placed on top of the oil, floating over the liquid until it is saturated with it. A short invocation is said to Oshún, asking that she intercede and force the man into marrying the petitioner. The lamp is lit every night at nine during five nights while repeating the invocation to Oshún. According to the santeros, this spell never fails.

TO DOMINATE A HUSBAND

The name of the husband is written on a piece of paper and placed inside a medium-sized, black or dark bottle, together with a used personal article, some ammonia, *esencia dominante,*

esencia amanza guapo, esencia de menta, and some of her urine.
The bottle is closed tightly and hid in a place where the victim
will not find it. Every time the husband becomes restless or
troublesome in any way, his wife simply shakes the bottle
several times. This simple act activates the magical ingredients
inside the bottle and gives her complete domination over her
husband.

FOR FERTILITY

A pomegranate is bought in the name of Yemayá, the beautiful
Yoruba moon goddess. She is the patroness of motherhood and
it is usually wise to enlist her aid in matters of fertility.
The pomegranate is cut in halves, which are both covered
with honey. A piece of paper with the name of the petitioner is
placed between the two halves of the pomegranate, which are
then put back together again. Yemayá is then invoked and asked
that in the same way the pomegranate is rich in health and
seeds, so will the petitioner be healthy and fruitful. A blue
candle is burned in Yemayá's honor every day for a month,
starting with the first day of the menstruation cycle. It is not
uncommon that women making this offer to this lovely goddess
become pregnant during this month.

TO DOMINATE A PERSON

This spell is used mostly for love, but it can be used to
overcome anybody. The name of the victim is written on a piece
of paper, which is then slowly wrapped in black thread. This is
accomplished by purchasing a spool of black thread on a Tuesday
and going for a long walk the same evening. As one walks, the
paper with the name is held in one hand, while with the other
one wraps the thread around the paper. By the time the spool
is empty, the paper should be completely covered by the thread
as by a black cocoon. The paper thus wrapped is thrown under
a bush or a tree and one returns home following a different
route.

TO SEPARATE A MAN AND A WOMAN

The names of the man and the woman are written on two separate pieces of paper and placed inside a bottle, together with the plant known as *morivivir*, some milk, and some vinegar. The santeros believe that in the same way the milk is made sour by the vinegar and the plant dies inside the bottle, so will the love between the two persons become sour and die. The bottle is buried in a place where the sun never reaches.

TO CREATE DIFFERENCES BETWEEN TWO PEOPLE

The names of the two persons are written on two separate pieces of paper and placed inside a glass of water. A piece of black cloth is tied over the glass top, which is then hidden in the farthest corner of the freezer. According to the santeros this spell would cause the end of the closest friendship or the most passionate love affair.

TO CREATE HATRED BETWEEN A MAN AND A WOMAN

Two black candles are bought in the shape of a man and a woman, respectively. The figures are inscribed with the names of the victims and sprinkled with the following powders:

odio	*voladores*
sal pa fuera	*precipitado rojo*
zorra	

The two figure candles are placed back to back and lit at midnight, starting on a Tuesday. The candles are allowed to burn a few minutes and are then snuffed out. The ritual is repeated every night during seven nights, moving the candles an inch apart from each other. On the last night of the seven, the candles are allowed to burn completely. The person who is doing this spell must remember to identify the two candles with the persons that he or she wants to separate.

TO DISPEL EVIL INFLUENCES

The Santeros recommend nine baths made with *pasote*, *anamú*, and *albahaca*. A white candle should be offered to Obatalá with each bath so that the orisha will clean away all evil vibrations.

TO DISPEL EVIL INFLUENCES

This traditional spell is worked out with the help of Saint Claire. An egg is placed inside a new glass that has been half filled with water. Saint Claire is invoked to bring about peace and harmony into one's life, and white candle is lit in her honor. This simple ritual is repeated during nine days. At the end of this period, the water from the glass is thrown into the street and the egg is brought to a park where it is crashed on the ground. Saint Claire is invoked again and asked that in the same way the egg was broken, so will evil disappear from one's life.

TO DISPEL EVIL INFLUENCES

This is a resguardo, a good-luck talisman, made with some garlic, *yerbabuena* and *perejil*. Some santeros recommend adding also a small piece of camphor, as evil spirits cannot resist the powerful smell of this substance. All the ingredients are placed in a small, homemade, white bag, which is then taken to seven churches and dipped into holy water. This bag is to be carried on one's person always to drive away negative influences.

TO PROTECT THE HOME

A simple protective device is to keep a sprig of *anamú*, tied with a red ribbon, behind every door.

TO PROTECT THE HOME

Some santeros place a cross of *tártago* behind their front door and underneath it they draw a cross with manteca de cacao.

TO ANNUL AN EVIL SPELL

The most rapid and effective way to annul an evil spell and send it back to its sender is to use the traditional "revocation" of Saint Michael.

A new glass is filled with water within an inch of the top. The glass is covered with a new saucer and turned upside down, ensuring that the water is not spilled and remains inside the glass, held by the saucer. Approximately an inch is cut from the top and the bottom of a white candle, allowing some of the wick to extend from the bottom part. The candle is then set upside down on the glass bottom and lit in the name of Saint Michael. The powerful archangel is then invoked and asked that in the same way the glass and the candle were reversed, so he will reverse the course of the enemy's spell and return it to its sender. The ritual is repeated during nine consecutive Tuesdays.

TO OVERCOME AN ENEMY

This spell requires the use of a piece of snake skin and some snake oil (*aceite de arrastrada*). The name of the enemy is written on a piece of parchment paper, which is then dipped in the snake oil. The paper is then sewn to the snake skin, which has been previously cut to fit the inside of a shoe. The snake skin is placed inside the shoe so that one is always stepping on the enemy's name. The symbolic meaning of the spell is that in the same way a snake crawls on the ground, so will the victim crawl at one's feet, powerless and humiliated.

TO OVERCOME AN ENEMY

Two cuts are made on a lime, one horizontally and the other vertically, ensuring that one does not cut the lime in four pieces. In the middle of the lime one places a piece of parchment paper with the victim's name written on it. The lime is then held closed with two long, steel pins, and placed in a new plain glass, together with some salt, vinegar, and ashes. The ashes and the salt are believed to destroy the enemy's attempts to cause trouble, while the lime and the vinegar will sour his own affairs.

TO OVERCOME AN ENEMY

A common practice is to place some pasote, sulfur, a lizard's tongue, and a used article of the victim on a yard of black cloth. All the materials are wrapped in the cloth, which is buried in the cemetery at the stroke of midnight. It is customary to leave a few coins over the small grave.

TO PACIFY AN ENEMY

It is recommended to boil four eggs and dip them in a mixture of *manteca de cacao, aceite de almendra* and *bálsamo tranquilo.* The eggs are then wrapped in a piece of white cotton and left under a large tree, preferably a ceiba or an oak tree. It is helpful to invoke Obatalá to help in pacifying and controlling the enemy.

TO GET RID OF AN ENEMY

One of the most effective spells is to sprinkle the following powders at the enemy's door: *polvos voladores, precipitado rojo,* garlic powder, cumin seed, salt, and some cigar ashes. The person thus bewitched will not last long at that address.

TO HARM AN ENEMY

For this purpose it is customary in Santería to wash a lodestone in dry wine and to sprinkle the wine on the door of the enemy, who will become sick shortly afterward.

FOR GOOD LUCK

Three despojos are prepared by boiling the following plants in a few gallons of water:

albahaca	three white roses
yerbabuena	three sprigs of *azucenas*
altamisa	

After the baths have been taken, the santeros recommend filling a small bowl with some honey and an egg yolk and keeping it under the bed during seven days. At this time the mixture is thrown away, preferably in the park. This helps to disperse bad luck and to attract good influences.

TO SOLVE A PROBLEM

A piece of paper with the description of the problem is placed inside a dark bottle, which is then filled with black coffee. The Seven African Powers are invoked so that they will dispose of the problem.

TO GET OR KEEP A JOB

This spell requires the help of the Seven African Powers. The first step is to purchase the working tools of the seven orishas. These are sold in a small envelope in most *botánicas*. It is also important to buy a nine-day candle of the type that has the name and image of the Seven African Powers stenciled on the glass in which it is encased. The candle is removed from the glass and anointed with the following oils: *aceite de triunfo, de dinero,* and *vencedor.* A piece of paper with the petitioner's name is placed at the bottom of the glass and the candle is replaced inside the glass. The candle is lit in the name of the Seven African Powers, and the tools are carried on one's person during the nine days the candle will burn. At the end of this time the tools are brought to a park and left underneath a tree or a large bush.

FOR GAMBLERS

The santeros recommend to all gamblers that they wash their hands with a bar of Gambler's soap before they engage in any game of chance. The use of special prebottled *despojos* for gamblers is also advised.

TO WIN A COURT CASE

On a cake of rough blue soap one writes the names of the court officials who will take part in the trial, and the name of the opponent. The soap is placed in a container of water and Elegguá is invoked to soften the minds and the wills of all the important people at the trial and to predispose them in one's behalf.

TO GAIN STRENGTH AND POWER

When the mayomberos are initiated they swallow seven grains of pepper with some holy water. Immediately afterward they eat the uncooked heart of a rooster. They believe this gives them unnatural strength and renders them immune to any disease or evil spell.

FOR GOOD HEALTH

A simple and reputedly effective practice is always to carry a small red bag containing seven grains of corn, dipped in *manteca de corojo*, and a small piece of camphor.

FOR GOOD HEALTH

It is believed to be good luck to carry a talisman known as *las muletas de San Lázaro*, which is a tiny gold-plated version of Saint Lazarus's crutches. Saint Lazarus is known in Santería as Babalú-Ayé, patron of the sick. It is also helpful to offer him a nine-day candle in exchange for good health. After the candle is consumed, the tiny crutches are left in the vicinity of a hospital.

FOR MONEY

A popular despojo for money is prepared by boiling *perejil, parami, yerba bruja, pacholi*, and five yellow roses in several gallons of water. Some honey and *esencia de dinero* are added to the bath after it has cooled. The despojo is used during five consecutive nights, asking Oshún for the money needed, and burning a yellow candle in her honor each of the five nights.

FOR MONEY

This unusual spell is to be used in case of bank loans or any type of financial transaction conducted through a bank. It is important, as the first step, to go to the bank that is handling the loan and get change for a dollar from one of the tellers. Five of the coins thus acquired are placed on a shallow saucer with the name of the bank written on a piece of paper under the coins. Five mint leaves are placed over the coins, and the saucer is then filled with *aceite intranquilo* and a bit of quicksilver. The wick and cork of a night light are set floating over the oil and lit for one hour every day at noon. According to the santeros, the bank officials will not rest until the loan has been successfully approved. It is very helpful to invoke Oshún's aid in this spell. The spell must be repeated during five days, starting the day the loan application is first signed.

Bibliography

Ajisafe, A.K. Laws and Customs of the Yoruba People. London. 1924.

Albertus Magnus. The Books of Secrets. London, circa 1560.

Baxter, Richard. The Certainty of the World of the Spirits. London, 1691.

Blumber, Martin F. A history of Amulets. Edinburgh, 1887.

Babin, Maria Teresa. Panorama de la Cultura Puertorriqueña. New York, 1958.

Bromhall, Thomas. A Treatise of Specters. London, 1658.

Buxton, T.F. The African Slave Trade. New York, 1893.

Cabrera, Lydia. El Monte. Miami, 1971.

_____. contes nègres de Cuba. Paris.

Constant, Alphonse. The Mysteries of Magic. A. E. Waite, ed., London, 1886.

Crowley, Aleister. Magick in Theory and Practice, New York, 1929.

Dorsainvil, J.C. Une explication philologique du vodou. Port-au-Prince, 1924.

Farrow, C.S. Faith. Fancies of Yoruba Paganism. London, 1924.

Frazer, James. The Golden Bough. London, 1890.

Freud, Sigmund. Totem and Taboo. New York, 1952.

Garcia Cortéz, Julio. El Santo (La Ocha). Miami, 1971.

Garrido, Pablo. Esoteria y Fervores Popularies de Puerto Rico. San Juan, 1942.

Graves, Robert. The White Goddess. New York, 1948.

Hughes, Pennethorne. Witchcraft. London, 1952.

Hurston, Zora. Voodoo Gods. London, 1939.

Iamblichus. De Mysteriis. London, Reprinted 1968.

Johnson, S. History of the Yorubas. London, 1921.

Jonas Sulfurino. El Libro de San Cipriano. Mexico, 1952.

Jung, Carl G. The Interpretation of Nature and the Psyche. London, 1955.

_____. Man and his Symbols. London, 1964.

_____. Mysterium Coniunctionis. New York, 1963.

_____. The Secret of the Golden Flower. New York and London, 1931.

_____. The Structure and Dynamics of the Psyche. New York, 1960.

Klein, H.S. Slavery in the Americas. New York, 1946.

Lachetenere, R. Oh mío Yemayá. Manzanillo, Cuba, 1938.

_____. El Sistema Religioso de los Lucumis y Otras Influencias Africanas en Cuba. Havana, 1940.

Leyel, C.F. The Magic of Herbs. New York, 1925.

Michaelis, Sebastian. A Discourse of Spirits. London, 1613.

Milburn, S. Magic and Charms of the Ijebu Province. London, 1932.

Ortiz, F. Brujos y Santeros. Havana, 1938.

Paracelsus. Selected Writings. Jolande Jacobi, ed., New York, 1951.

Pavitt, D., Kate, A., and Thomas, W. The Book of Talismans, Amulets and

Zodiacal Gems. London, 1914.
Ramos, A. Introduçao a Anthropologia Brasileira. Rio de Janeiro, 1943.
————. O Negro na Civilizaçao Brasileira. Rio de Janeiro, 1956.
Rhine, J.B. The Reach of the Mind. London. 1948.
Rigaud, Milo. Secrets of Voodoo. New York, 1970.
Robbins, Russell Hope. Encyclopedia of Witchcraft and Demonology. London, 1959.
Rogers, Andrés R. Los Caracoles. New York, 1973.
Rosario, J.C., and Carrion, J. Problemas Sociales, El Negro en Haiti, Los Estados Unidos, Puerto Rico. San Juan, 1940.
Verger, P. Dieux d'Afrique. Paris, 1928.
Verger, P. Flux et reflux de la traite des nègres. Paris, 1917.
Willlam, J.J. Voodoos and Obcahs, Phases of West Indies Witchcraft. New York, 1933.
Wren, R.C. Potter's New Encyclopedia of Botanical Drugs and Preparations. Sussex, 1917.
Wyndham. Myths of Life. London, 1921.

Glossary

Abakoso-Changó title of Changó
Aberínku nonbeliever
Abikú mischievous spirit that reincarnates in a human child who dies in early childhood
aceite amarra hombre oil used in love spells
aceite de almendra almond oil
aceite de amor love oil
aceite de arrastrade snake oil
aceite de coco coconut oil
aceite de dendé special oil used in Brazil in magic spells
aceite de lirio lily oil
aceite de menta mint oil
aceite de triunfo oil used to attain victory in any human endeavor
aceite intranquilo restless oil
aceite vencedor oil of triumph used to overcome enemies
aceite yo puedo y tu no oil "I can but you cannot"
aché grace, power
acheré instrument used to invoke the gods
afoché special powder made with the ashes of a chicken
afochés ritualistic dances of the Negroes of Rio de Janeiro
Aganyú diety of volcanoes
agbebé fan used to help cool the orishas when they become angry
aggueni peacock
agogó instrument used to invoke the gods
ajenjo a plant used for medicinal teas, especially stomach upsets
Ajigbona a second order of babalawos
Akoñrín singer or caller of the orishas
akoyú wise man

akumí native of Aku
alabbgwanna the lonely spirit
Alafi-Changó another title of Changó
alafia one of the positions of the coconut divination system
alaroye an Elegguá
alabahaca an herb used for medicinal purposes and in depojos
aleyo nonbeliever
altamisa artemisa
amalá food offered to Changó
amanza guapo oil or essence used to overcome a person. It means "overcome the strong."
amarre spell
amoníaco (armoníaco) ammonia
amor an oil, powder, or essence used in love spells. It means "love."
Anagui one of the aspects of Elggua
anamú (petiveria alliacea) plant used as an abortive and to dispel evil
ancori singing
Aphrodite Greek goddess of love and beauty
araba sacred tree of Santería (ceiba)
Ares Greek god of war
Aroni god of medicine
Artemis Greek goddess of the moon and hunters
artemisa plant used by the santeros to cure appendicitis and in purifying baths
asiento initiation ceremony
atabaques sacred ritual drum in Brazil
atractiva oil, essence or powders used in love spells
Aye or **Aya** midget goddess of the jungle
Ayeru an Elegguá
Ayé-Shaluga god of fortune and good

luck
azucenas tropical variety of lilies
azufre sulfur

babalawo high priest of Santería
Babalú-Ayé patron of the sick
bálsamo tranquilo peace balm
bámbula dance
Bantu African tribe
Baraine an Elegguá
batá the three ritualistic drum used in the ceremonies of Santería
bilongo evil spell
Binah the third station of the Tree of Life.
bohíos peasant huts in Puerto Rico
botánicas religious goods stores which are the center of operations for the santeros
boumba an nganga prepared without the cauldron
brujería witchcraft
brujo witch

caballeros knights
cabildos meetings where the laws and rites of Santería are taught to the initiates
Caña fístola a type of cane used for medicinal purposes
canastillero small cabinet where the santero keeps the otanes and other magical implements
candomblé Yoruba rites in Brazil
caracoles seashells
cararu soup
cascarilla powdered eggshell
ceiba sacred tree of Santería
Changó god of fire, thunder, and lightning
Chankpana god of smallpox
cheketé traditional drink of the guemilere
Chesed the fourth station of the Tree of Life

Chiyidi god of nightmares
Chokmah the second station of the Tree of Life
chula frog
ciudad de los brujos city of witches
coitre blanco a plant used for medicinal purposes
collares bead neclaces used by the santeros
Congos the name given in Latin America to the members of the Bantu tribe
Dada god of unborn children and of gardens
darle coco al santo give coconut to the saint (divination procedure using four pieces of coconut)
derecho "sacred" money paid by the initiate to his or her sponsor during the asiento
despacho magic spell in Brazil
despojo herbal bath to dispel evil influences and to attract good luck
despojo de amor love bath
diablitos de P.R. little devils of Puerto Rico
diloggun or **mediloggun** the Table of Ifá
dodobale a ritual of Santería, usually conducted after the asiento
dominante an oil or essence used to overcome a person. It means "dominant."
Dona Janaina Yemayá in Brazil

ebbó protective spell
ebó Brazilian term for the magical practices of Santuario
El Anima Sola the lonely spirit
Eleda guardian angel of the head
Elegguá messenger of the gods; he stands behind doors and opens or closes the way to opportunity
elekes protective head necklace of

the cult

Ellife one of the positions of the coconut divination system

esencia de amor love essence

esencia dominante dominant essence

Elufe an aspect of Elegguá

enkangar to cast a spell

enviación a destructive spell that uses a "hired" spirit to harm an enemy

escoba amarga (partenium hysterophorus) plant used in purifying baths and to drive away the abikús

esencia amanza guapo essence "to overcome the strong," also in oil

esencia amarra hombre man-binder essence; also available in oil

esencia atractiva "attractive" and powder

esencia de dinero money essence

esencio de la buena suerte good luck essence

esencia de mosca musk essence, also available in oil and powder

esencia imán lodestone essence, also available in oil and powder

esencia vencedora triumphant essence

Eshu an aspect of Elegguá

Eshu alayiki an Elegguá, bringer of the unexpected

Eshu Bi an Elegguá who stands in the corners

Eshu Ogguanilebbe an aspect of Elegguá

Eshu oku oro an Elegguá who controls life and death

Espíritu Dominante the Dominant Spirit

Espíritu Intranquilo the Restless Spirit

espíritu travieso poltergeist

estera straw mat where the sea-shells are read

ewe Yoruba term for herbs

exorcism the act of banishing an evil spirit

Exu Eshu in Brazil

eyá a room inside the ileocha or temple

eyé blood

ezulu heaven

fiestas de santo ceremonies or celebrations in honor of the saints

filhas-de-santo ceremonies or celebrations in honor of the saints

foribale genuflexion made in front of the drums or the sanctuary

fula gun powder

fundamento foundation

gan-gán huge

Geburah the fifth station of the Tree of Life

guano bendito palm leaves given by the Catholic church on Palm Sunday

guao poison ivy

Guayama the city of witches in Puerto Rico

güemilere sacred ceremony of Santería

güiro gourd of the tropics

gurunfinda talisman of a mayombero

gwagwa o dé crossing of four roads

hacer el santo initiation ceremony

Helios Greek god of the sun

Hermes messenger of the gods in Greek mythology

higuereta (ricinus communis) plant from which castor oil is processed

Hod the eighth station of the Tree of Life

ibán-balo backyard of the temple

Ibeyi twin gods who protect infants

Ifá god of impossible things
igbodu sanctuary where the talismans and stones of the orishas are kept
Iggi-olorun the ceiba among the mayomberos
ikú death
ilé house
Ile Ife holy city where Yemayá died
ileocha temple where ceremonies are held
incubus, incubi male spirit(s) that seek to mate with living women
irawo stars
iré good luck
iroko sacred tree of Santería (ceiba)
irolé day in Yoruba language
iruke special feather duster used to banish evil spirits
Itagua one of the positions of the coconut divination system
italero a santero or babalawo who specializes in reading the "Table of Ifá"
Iyáa Eve of the Yoruba myth
Iya Agbe Oduddúa as the blind mother
iyalocha santera

Jupiter one of the seven planets of ancient astrologers; father of the gods in Roman mythology jutia possum

kamba broom
Kether the first station of the Cabalistic Tree of Life
kisanguele snake used by the mayombero
kisengue human tibia used as a sceptre by mayombero
kiyumba cadaver used by the mayombre to make the nganga
Kronos greek god of time
kuna place

Las Mercedes Our Lady of Mercy
las muletas de San Lázaro St. Lazarus's crutches
Las Siete Potencias Africanas The Seven African Powers
lavándula roja red lavender
libretas handwritten notebooks where the santero keeps his spell and invocations
lirio oil used in love spells
locas men dress as women
Loción de Pompeya Lotion of Pompeii, a common ingredient of love spells
Lóiza Aldea city in Puerto Rico where the traditional feast of St. James is celebrated
Lonely Spirit Alabbgwana; used by the snateros in desperate cases, especially love problems

macumba Brazilian Santería
macuto the sack where the boumba is kept
madrina "godmother" or sponsor of the yaguo
mae d'agua mother of waters in Brazil
makuto resguardo, talisman
malembé care, cautiousness
Malkuth the tenth station of the Tree of Life
mamá Cachita Oshún
mamá Ungundu the ceiba among the mayomberos
maná a leaf used for medicinal purposes
manteca de cacao cocoa butter
manteca de corojo special vegetable grease used by the santeros in their ceremonies and spells
Mars one of the seven planets of ancient astrologers; god of war among the Romans, symbol of strength

masango evil spell
mastuerzo a popular ingredient for
love spells
mayombero practitioner of palo
mayombe, a black witch
mbua evil spirit used in a spell
mejorana marjoram
menta mint
Mercury one of the seven planets of
ancient astrologers; symbolizes
messages, papers, intellectual endeavors
moddu cué thank you
Moon one of the seven planets of the
ancient astrologers; symbolizes in-
tuition, mother image
morivivir special plant used in love
spells
mpambu four cardinal points
mpungo Congo god
mundele white person

Ndoki the most evil of all the ngangas
Netzach the seventh station of the
Tree of Life
nfinda Kalunga cemetery
nganga a big evil spell; also the
mayombero's cauldron
ngua a call to a familiar spirit
nitro dulce a plant used to cure
dysentery
nkangue binding spell (bilongo)
nkisi spirit
nkunia casa sami tree house of God
(ceiba)
npaka an animal horn used to force a
spirit to manifest itself
nsambi God
nsambi kuna ezulu God is in heaven
nsambi kuna ntoto God is in earth
nsasi palm tree
ntoto earth
nzalim the lightning bolt

obba king among the Yorubas

Oba wife of Changó
Obafulom the Adam of the Yoruba
myth
Obatalá major Yoruba deity and father of the gods
obi coconut
obi gui gui dry coconut
Ocana-Sode one of the positions of
the coconut divination system
Ochosi god of the unters of birds and
wild animals
Ochu at one time she was the moon
goddess
Ochukowa oro waning moon
Ochumare goddess of the rainbow
oddániko a severe beating with a
leather crop, used in cases of false
possessions
óddara aggadágoddo very strong
odduarás flintstones
Oddudúa wife of Obatalá
odofin substitutes for the babalawo in
his absence
ogbo concoction, brew
Oggún god of war and iron
ojuani one of the positions in the
seashell divination system
Oke god of mountains
okkuó dead
okoni teacher
Olarosa protector of homes
Olimerin protector of villages
Olodumare God
Olodumare Nzame one of the aspects of God
Olofi one of the aspects of God, who
is the earth's guardian
Olokun hermaphrodite god
olokun-Yemayá goddess of the ocean
depths
Olorun-Olofi God, the creator of the
universe
Olosa favorite concubine of Olokun
oluwo the highest degree among
babalawos

omiero liquid used by the santeros during their initiation ceremonies

omo-Changó a santero devoted to Changó

Omo-Oba (Olosi) the first man, created by Olodumare

Omo-Oggún santero devoted to Oggun

omo-orisha santero devoted to a specific orisha

Omo-Oshún santero devoted to Oshún

oddi one of the patterns used in seashell divination

oddun any of the patterns of the seashells that are used in the divination system of Santería

oggunda one of the positions in seashell divination system

ori head

oriate master of ceremonies

orisha Yoruba god or goddess

Orisha-Oka god of fields and harvests

Orixalá Obatalá in Brazil

oru series of invocationns

Orun god of the sun

Orungán son of Aganyú and Yemayá

Orúnla or **Orunmila** owner of the Table of Ifá

Orunmila Orúnla

Osachin patron of doctors; his symbol is a bird of prey

Osain god of herbs

Osanyin god of medicine

Oshún goddess of love, marriage, and gold

Osun one of the warrior gods usually represented by a small iron rooster

otán special stone sacred to an orisha

owó money

Oyá goddess of fire, patroness of justice

Oyé giant god of storms

Oyekun one of the positions of the coconut divination system

Oxalá Obatala in Brazil

pacholi patchouli

pai-de-Santo Brazilian santero

palo mayombe the black magic of the Congos

palo monte one of the branches or sects of Congo magic

parada part of the asiento when the yaguo collapses on the floor while being possessed by his orisha

parami special herb used in despojos and for good luck

paraiso herb used for good luck and to dispel evil

pasote an herb used in despojos

pedrega sandy substance used in a plaster to mend broken bones

pegis special altar for an orisha in Brazil

perejil parsley, used in resguardos and despojos

petate straw mats used by peasants in Puerto Rico

poltergeist a mischievous spirit that creates visible supernatural phenomena

polvo de imán lodestone powder

polvos de odio "hatred" powder

polvos de zorra powders used to harm an enemy

polvos voladores powder used to get rid of an enemy

precipitado rojo extremely powerful powder used to harm an enemy

prenda endearing term used by the mayombero to describe the nganga

rainha do mar queen of the seas in Brazil

registro consultation

resguardo good luck talisman, believed to protect its wearer against evil

revocación de cabeza spiritual and

ritualistic cleansing of the head
revocation of Saint Michael a powerful counter spell
riegos special liquid sprinkled throughout the house to dispel evil influences
rompe zaraguey plant used to dispel evil
rosa de Jericó Jerico rose

sahumerio fumes used to dispel evil influences
sal de violeta violet salts
sal pa fuera powder used to get rid of an enemy
santero, santera practitioner of Santería
Santiago Apostol Saint James
santigüo a curative system used by the santero by means of which he "blesses" the body of a sick person and dispels all evil influence
santo saint
santo lavados simpler initiation ceremony where a person may receive some of the powers of an orisha
Santuario Santería in Brazil
Saturn one of the seven planets of ancient astrologers; controls time and is a symbol of wisdom
sebo de Flande tallow grease
Seven African Powers, The a group of the seven most powerful orishas of Santería, namely, Obatalá, Changó, Oggún, Orúnla, Yemayá, Oshún, and Elegguá
sígueme an oil or essence used in love spells. It means "follow me."
soperas bowls where the stones are kept
succubus, succubi female spirit(s) that seek to make with living men
suelda con suelda an herb used to mend broken bones

Sun one of the seven planets of ancient astrologers; symbol of fire

Table of Ifá divination system of Santería that employs seashells
Takata god of stones
talako albino
tártago herb used to dispel evil
Tata Nkisi mayombero
telemene to spy
telemense nkisi an order to a spirit to spy on somebody
terreiros temples of Santería in Brazil
Tiphareth the sixth station of the Tree of Life

uenba evil spell
umbanda the Brazilian equivalent of Congo magic
una Gota de Amor a love perfume
unyéun livelihood

valeriana an herb used in love spells
vegigantes little devils of Puerto Rico
vencedora an essence used in love spells
vente conmigo an oil or essence used in love spells. It means "Come with me."
Venus one of the seven planets of ancient astrologers; symbol of beauty and love
verdolaga purslane
viejos old men
vititi nfinda Congo term for herbs

Xangó Changó in Brazil

yaguó initiate of Santería
ya nijila an apology
yaya mother
yemanjá Yemayá in Brazil
Yemayá daughter of Obatalá and Oddudúa, and the Yoruba moon

goddess who controls the seas and the water element

Yemayá Achabbá Yemayá as a very demanding goddess

Yemayá Ataramagwa sarabbi olokun Yemayá as the majestic queen of the seas

Yemayá Attraramawa Yemayá in her most proud and arrogant aspect

Yemayá Oggute Yemayá in one of most violent and virile aspects

Yemmu Obatalá'o wife

yerbabuena mentha sativa; used in medicinal teas and in despojos

yerba bruja a powerful herb used for medicinal purposes and for despojos

yerba dulce an herb used in love spells

yerba linda a sweet smelling herb used in love spells and despojos

Yerba mora (salanum nigrum) used medicinally as a tea for calming nerves

Yesod the ninth station of the Tree of Life

Yeyé-Cari Oshún

Yeye-mara Oshún

yeza tribal marks of the Yoruba

Yo puedo y tu no an oil or essence used to overcome a person. It mean "I can and you cannot."

Yoruba African tribe whose myths and rites are the basis of Santería

yubbona sponsor of the yaguó

zarabanda a stype of nganga, also a powerful Congo diety

Zeus father of the gods in Greek mythology

zun zún an herb used in love spells

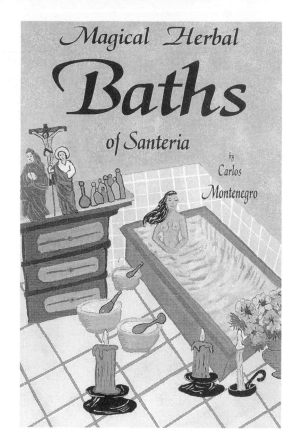

MAGICAL HERBAL BATHS OF SANTERIA
by Carlos Montenegro

One of the reasons that Santeria has become so popular is due to the use of natural remedies and herbal medicines prepared by the Santero Priests. By combining elements of spirituality with that of nature, a Santero Priest can accomplish great success with even the most difficult case. Spiritual herbal baths are widely used in the Santeria religion. Although all of the ingredients are natural, when combined with powerful supernatural magic, these herbal baths can produce incredible results. Spiritual baths have been used for hundreds of years to heal sickness and for supernatural power. The Montenegro Family has been practicing Santeria for over 200 years. This book explores the mysteries and techniques of preparing herbal baths used in traditional Santeria. The book contains lists of herbs, oils, powders, rituals and other magical ingredients used by Santeros for hundreds of years. *Orisha baths, love baths, money baths, cleansing baths, sweet baths and also baths used in Palo Mayombe and traditional Mexican witchcraft.* $5.95

RITUALS and SPELLS
of SANTERÍA
by Migene González-Wippler

Santería is an earth religion. That is, it is a magico-religious system that has its roots in nature and natural forces. Each orisha or saint is identified with a force of nature and with a human interest or endeavor Chango, for instance, is the god of fire, thunder and lightning, but he is also the symbol of justice and protects his followers against enemies. He also symbolizes passion and virility and is often invoked in works of seduction. Oshun, on the other hand, symbolizes river waters, love and marriage. She is essentially the archetype of joy and pleasure. Yemaya is identified with the seven seas, but is also the symbol of Motherhood and protects women in their endeavors. Elegguá symbolizes the crossroads, and is the orisha of change and destiny, the one who makes things possible or impossible. He symbolizes the balance of things. Obatalá is the father, the symbol of peace and purity. Oyá symbolizes the winds and is the owner of the cemetery, the watcher of the doorway between life and death. She is not death, but the awareness of its existence. Oggún is the patron of all metals, and protects farmers, carpenters, butchers, surgeons, mechanics, and all who work with or near metals. He also rules over accidents, which he often causes.

Many rituals and spells are included in this book, such as, To Break an Evil Spell, For Good Luck, To Attract Men, To Make a Person Return, To Make a Person Leave, these and many others to help you with all your needs.

5 1/2"x8", 134 pages, paperback $6.95

ISBN 0-942272-07-2

SANTERÍA
FORMULARY & SPELLBOOK

CANDLES • HERBS • INCENSE • OILS
A GUIDE TO NATURE'S MAGIC

CARLOS MONTENEGRO

ITEM #039
$14.95

The belief in natural magic is shared by millions who are participants of the Afro Caribbean religion known as Santeria. This book was written as a *"How to"* guide for individuals who are active participants in the Santeria Religion. It's purpose is to introduce and encourage individuals of Santeria to familiarize themselves with an inexpensive way of preparing basic ingredients to produce "natural magic". Rarely is careful attention paid to the preparation of homemade magic products in these modern times. Rarer still, is finding an individual who is dedicated and competent in this aspect of spellcrafting. It is a magical institution that is dying and must not be overlooked or forgotten. Making homemade products is a lengthy process, but the success of a magical spell or ritual demands patience and faith. This book is an important resource guide to the magic found within nature. If properly utilized with respect and reverence, the Santeria practitioner will live harmoniously in nature with the Orishas.

POWERS OF THE ORISHAS

Santeria and the Worship of Saints

Migene Gonzalez Wippler

Item #005 - $8.95

Santeria is the Afro-Cuban religion based on an amalgamation between some of the magio-religious beliefs and practices of the Yoruba people and those of the Catholic church. In Cuba where the Yoruba proliferated extensively, they became known as *Lucumi,* a word that means "friendship".

Santeria is known in Cuba as Lucumi Religion. The original Yoruba language, interspersed with Spanish terms and corrupted through the centuries of misuse and mispronunciation, also became known as Lucumi. Today some of the terms used in Santeria would not be recognized as Yoruba in Southwestern Nigeria, the country of origin of the Yoruba people.

Santeria is a Spanish term that means a confluence of saints and their worship. These saints are in reality clever disguises for some of the Yoruba deities, known as Orishas. During the slave trade, the Yoruba who were brought to Cuba were forbidden the practice of their religion by their Spanish masters. In order to continue their magical and religious observances safely the slaves opted for the identification and disguise of the Orishas with some of the Catholic saints worshipped by the Spaniards. In this manner they were able to worship their deities under the very noses of the Spaniards without danger of punishment.

Throughout the centuries the practices of the Yoruba became very popular and soon many other people of the Americas began to practice the new religion.